ALL ABOUT
REAL ESTATE
INVESTING

Other Titles in the "All About..." Series

ALL ABOUT REAL ESTATE INVESTING

The Easy Way to Get Started

WILLIAM BENKE
JOSEPH M. FOWLER

Second Edition

McGraw-Hill

New York   Chicago   San Francisco   Lisbon   London   Madrid
Mexico City   Milan   New Delhi   San Juan   Seoul
Singapore   Sydney   Toronto

Library of Congress Cataloging-in-Publication Data

Benke, William.
    All about real estate investing : the easy way to get started / by William Benke and
Joseph M. Fowler.—2nd ed.
        p.   cm.
    ISBN 0-07-137431-0
    1. Real estate investment.   I. Fowler, Joseph M.   II. Title.

    HD1382.5.B46 2001
    332.63'24—dc21

                                                                    2001018053

McGraw-Hill

A Division of The **McGraw·Hill** Companies

This book was set in Palatino per the IPROF design specs by Joanne Morbit and
Paul Scozzari of McGraw-Hill's Hightstown, N.J., Professional Book Group com-
position unit.

Printed and bound by R. R. Donnelley & Sons Company.

McGraw-Hill books are available at special discounts to use as premiums and sales
promotions, or for use in corporate training programs. For more information,
please write to the Director of Special Sales, Professional Publishing, McGraw-Hill,
Two Penn Plaza, New York, NY 10121-2298. Or contact your local bookstore.

This publication is designed to provide accurate and authoritative information in
regard to the subject matter covered. It is sold with the understanding that the pub-
lisher is not engaged in rendering legal, accounting or other professional service.
If legal advice or other expert assistance is required, the services of a competent
professional person should be sought.
—*From a declaration of principles jointly adopted by a committee of the American Bar
Association and a committee of publishers.*

This book is printed on recycled, acid-free paper containing a
minimum of 50% recycled de-inked fiber.

CONTENTS

PREFACE

Real estate offers excellent investment opportunities. But for most individuals, real estate investment is not the get-rich-quick panacea that the multitude of seminar promoters would have us believe. One must question why so many self-proclaimed multi-millionaire seminar hosts devote such a disproportionate level of time and energy to real estate seminars and related sales rather than to real estate investment itself.

Nevertheless, many great fortunes have been started in real estate by individuals with only modest resources. Such success, however, has usually been the result of good investment decisions rather than unique schemes. Real estate investment decisions involve a process that is not dissimilar from that required for other types of investment. The investor must understand the factors influencing profitability, assemble quantitative data concerning these factors, and then translate the data into an assessment of probable profitability and attendant risk.

Accordingly, a primary focus of this book is profitability assessment—the bottom line for any investment decision. In the case of real estate, it is often done very poorly. This is due in part to the multitude of variables that describe real estate investment scenarios, including the buy terms (price, down payment, interest rate, contract period), the sell terms (similar variables), the hold period between buy and sell, the expected appreciation rate, the expenses incurred to carry the property, the income produced, etc.

These variables complicate a realistic assessment of expected profitability. However, unless such assessment is accurately performed, an intelligent investment decision is not possible. Does this mean that real estate investors must be accomplished financial analysts? Not at all. In this age of computers, most real estate firms are equipped to provide such service, given the proper inputs concerning the variables involved. However, investors must be sufficiently knowledgeable concerning the fundamentals in order to arrange for and input appropriate analysis, assess its validity, and properly interpret the results.

To assist in this process, we have included a unique series of charts for rental houses, apartments, and land that permit the investor to screen properties of interest for potential profitability prior to a more precise or extensive analysis. All that is required is to gather together certain basic information concerning the variables that describe the real estate investment scenario under consideration, and then use the charts to translate this information into an estimate of expected rate of return on investment.

While the book is written to accommodate less experienced real estate investors, the profitability analysis charts will be an invaluable reference source for even the most sophisticated investor in screening real estate investment opportunities.

Other important subjects covered include the characteristics of different types of real estate investment (rental houses, apartments, land), selection considerations, use of the Internet in real estate investing, individual vs. group investing, the impacts of inflation, things you need to understand about real estate brokers, tenant considerations, financing strategies, and negotiating strategies and tactics that will further enhance prospects for a successful outcome.

ALL ABOUT REAL ESTATE INVESTING

CHAPTER 1

Why Real Estate?

Real estate has both advantages and disadvantages over other investment options. The best option, of course, is largely an individual matter dictated by investor compatibility. Factors that determine compatibility include personality, temperament, interests, risk tolerance, and overall financial status. The high-risk, volatile investment environment that characterizes commodities may be fine for some but totally unsuited for others. Similarly, the conservative, fixed-income investment approach has its place for a specific segment of society. Nevertheless, real estate continues to be an option well worth considering—either as a primary investment focus or as part of a diversified investment portfolio.

One of the primary appeals of real estate investment is that it provides an excellent opportunity to leverage investment funds. *Leverage* is simply the extent to which credit is used to finance the investment. Leverage pays off because it permits the investor to tie up property at a fraction of its total value and to take advantage of the depreciating value of the dollars used to pay off the debt. Leverage is one of the advantages of real estate over investments that require payment in full at the time of purchase. Leverage is not unique to real estate; it can also be used in the purchase of securities and commodities. However, real estate tends to be much more stable and less volatile than most other investment types that offer the opportunity to employ leverage. More on leverage later.

Second, real estate is appealing because of the relatively high rate at which it has historically appreciated in value compared to inflation. In order to make a financial gain by the use of borrowed funds, the item purchased must appreciate in value at a rate that exceeds that of inflation and the interest paid on the funds borrowed (which is a function of inflation). For example, if the annual interest rate is 8 percent on funds borrowed to finance the purchase of property that inflates in value at 10 percent each year, the result is a net annual gain of 2 percent. This oversimplification obviously fails to take into account a number of other relevant factors such as tax implications, fees, carrying costs, and the timing of payments and receipts, but it nevertheless illustrates the point. Good real estate has generally met this criterion over time.

In some years, real estate has taken a "hit" and declined in value in parts of the United States. In this respect, real estate is like most investment categories that experience up and down cycles, and such slumps must be viewed in a longer term context. In areas of growing population, real estate has generally appreciated at rates substantially exceeding those of inflation. Its long-term prospects remain positive and, as in most investments, down periods typically represent the best buying opportunities. There is a general feeling among many economists today that inflation may have bottomed, making real estate an increasingly attractive investment opportunity for the decade ahead.

Among the fundamentals that influence this view is the fact that available land area remains relatively fixed while urban concentration patterns and resulting supply and demand pressures will continue to exert upward pressures on desirable real estate. Most of projected U.S. population growth over the foreseeable future will be highly concentrated around urban population centers. Pressures on real estate prices will be further amplified by escalating environmental regulations. Still other pressures include the growing world demand for U.S. food and agricultural products, significant levels of investment by foreign parties in U.S. properties, and continuing demand for second home purchases and recreational developments.

Third, real estate is an appealing investment because of the tax advantages it provides. The deductibility of interest from taxable income lowers the effective borrowing cost of money. This is discussed more fully in Chapter 2. Depreciation charge-offs are another tax shelter benefit applicable to improved property. Land is not depreciable, but buildings and other structures are. Tax laws permit depreciation of the value of such property over time. In effect, the tax laws assume that depreciable property diminishes in value each year due to obsolescence or deterioration. This yearly paper loss can be charged as a deductible expense against income that would otherwise be taxed. In reality, there is no cash flow loss, but rather a theoretical reduction in value. However, it is treated as though it were a cash flow expense and therefore reduces the taxable income each year during the period over which the property is held.

On the negative side, depreciation contributes to a larger taxable gain at the time of sale since the cost basis is the purchase price and related fees plus any improvements to the property less the depreciation claimed over the period it is held. The day of tax payment reckoning therefore comes when the property is sold. The gain at that time is defined as the difference between the income derived from sale of the property and the cost basis, as defined above. Nevertheless, the tax that must ultimately be paid on the gain is deferred until resale and is at a capital gains rate. A tax payment deferred on a no-interest basis equates to value, of course, since the funds made available during the interim have earning potential through other investment opportunities.

In considering the tax consequences of real estate, it is important to keep in mind the passive-loss rules that may be in effect. At the time of this writing, these rules say that losses from passive activities can offset only income from passive activities. Excess passive losses are suspended until a future date when such losses can be offset by passive income or when the activity is relinquished (at which time losses can offset any type of income). Real estate rental is considered a passive activity. There is, however, up to a $25,000 annual loss deduction from the passive-loss limit permitted to individuals who actively participate in real estate rental activities. Refer to your federal income tax guide for specifics on this because the allowable deduction may be less or not applicable, depending on a number of factors concerning marital status and whether separate or joint returns are filed. This limit applies only if the individual's adjusted gross income does not exceed $100,000. There are reduced allowances when adjusted gross income exceeds this level. An active participant is one who owns more than 10 percent of the property and is a bona fide and significant participant in management decisions or in the hiring of third parties to maintain the property. In effect, investment in real estate rentals typically qualifies as a nonprofessional sideline.

Fourth, real estate is appealing in that it permits retention of control by the investor. You, the investor, make your own decisions throughout the investment cycle. Unlike many investments where the expertise of a professional agent is essential, the real estate investor can be the captain of his or her own ship, deciding what and when to buy, when to sell, what improvements to make, and the host of other decisions that are involved during the investment cycle. By its very nature, real estate is influenced in value primarily by local circumstances and conditions. National or international political and economic trends do have an influence, but are much less direct and important than local or regional circumstances. The expertise required involves effort, but of a type that is relatively easy to develop. The basic principles mentioned and the investment charts provided in this book will provide many of the essential tools to invest intelligently. A primary advantage enjoyed by the professional over the nonprofessional real estate investor is exposure to opportunities. However, since real estate agents cannot purchase all of the desirable opportunities that emerge, they may be regarded as a useful resource rather than undue competition.

Finally, real estate is appealing because it satisfies one of the fundamental human needs of society. These needs include food, clothing, shelter, protection, transportation, energy, and medical care. Regardless of the changes in the nation's economy or its monetary system, these elements are essential to life and the basic structure of society. They represent real value and provide the reference against which the worth of less essential items are ultimately measured and indexed. Investments oriented toward such basics are therefore assured a measure of safety and stability that cannot usually be found in many other forms of investment.

Balanced against these positive aspects, the investor must keep in mind some of the drawbacks to real estate compared with other investment options. One of these is reduced liquidity. It takes longer to sell real estate than stocks, bonds, or commodities.

Income property brings with it the headaches associated with tenants—selection, rent collection, evictions, damage to property, clean-up between tenants, maintenance—and a host of other ongoing management functions. Unlike most other investment options, searching out and locating good investment opportunities in real estate requires a significant investment in time and effort. And, unlike many other investments, real estate is particularly prone to governmental intervention through regulations rooted in environmental protection.

These drawbacks, of course, apply to those who are actually involved in selecting and managing the investment properties. For those not so inclined, a passive approach remains a possibility through ownership in such managed real estate entities as REITs (real estate investment trusts), limited partnerships, and other forms of group investment discussed in Chapter 11.

CHAPTER 2

Better a Debtor Be!

An understanding of inflation in terms of its implications concerning various types of investments is important simply because some investments fare extremely well under an inflationary environment while others do not. If you believe that even modest inflation levels will characterize the future, then investments that generally benefit under such an environment should receive serious consideration. Even in the event of a period of slow economic growth, it is not likely that inflation will disappear entirely. Real estate is somewhat unique in that it provides favorable opportunities under most economic environments, although it is particularly desirable as a hedge against inflation.

CREDITORS VERSUS DEBTORS

Inflation takes a toll upon creditors in that it reduces the value of claims to fixed amounts of money. The debtor, on the other hand, gains since he pays off his debts in depreciated or "cheap" money. We usually think of creditors as those who have made loans to others. In reality, however, most of us are creditors as well as debtors. For example, if you hold a life insurance policy, own bonds, or have a savings account, you are a creditor. You have invested funds under agreements that promise the return of these funds (or its equivalent value in services) at some specified future date, along with some additional dollar premium or service that constitutes the gain to you in exchange for the investment of your funds. The creditor loses if his claim is settled with depreciated currency. The creditor's loss, of course, is the debtor's gain. In effect the latter pays his debts in dollars that have a reduced value from that which existed at the time the agreement was made. In addition to our role as creditors through savings accounts, investments, and life insurance policies, most of us are also debtors to the extent that we have long-term mortgages on our homes, and we finance automobiles, appliances, and a wide range of other purchases with short- to medium-term payment plans.

The tendency for extended periods of inflation to hurt lenders and benefit borrowers, and to redistribute wealth in such a manner as to cause this result, is further aggravated by existing tax laws. While laws are always subject to change, it is likely that they will continue to favor the borrower at the expense of the lender. The reason that tax laws aggravate inflationary impacts is quite simple. As inflation increases, interest rates also rise in order to compensate the lender for inflation and still provide a real return. *Real return* refers to the return which is in excess of inflation, or stated another way, the increase in purchasing power realized by the lender after his investment or loan has been recovered, along with the interest or gain generated. However, such a definition ignores the impact of taxes. Interest receipts are taxable, and the lender pays proportionately more taxes on his earned interest as inflation increases. For example, in an environment where the average inflation rate is 2 percent, assume that a typical lender decides that he must earn a 3 percent real gain on his funds in order to receive adequate compensation for the risk involved in a particular situation, as noted in Case 1. He would probably charge an interest rate of 5 percent (2 percent to compensate for inflation plus 3 percent for real gain). Assume now that the annual inflation rate increases to 5 percent (Case 2). In order for the lender to continue to net a real gain of 3 percent on the same type of loan, he would presumably find it necessary to charge an interest rate of 8 percent annually (5 percent to compensate for inflation plus 3 percent, as before, for real gain). However, examine the after-tax results, assuming that the lender is in a 31 percent income tax bracket:

	Case 1	Case 2
Interest rate charge on loan	5.0%	8.0%
Less portion used to pay income taxes (31% bracket)	(1.6%)	(2.5%)
Less erosion due to inflation	(2.0%)	(5.0%)
After-tax rate of real return	1.4%	0.5%

In this illustration, the lender's real return under the higher infla-tion rate (Case 2) dropped to one-third of that previously earned under a lower inflation rate (Case 1), even though he had raised the interest rate, presumably to adequately compensate for the increased inflation. The erosion in his real return resulted from the proportionately larger tax bite he suffered under the higher infla-tion situation.

It is apparent, therefore, that current tax laws amplify the ero-sive impact of inflation from the standpoint of the creditor or lender. But what about the debtor or borrower? Do the tax laws fur-ther enhance or reduce the general benefits that he or she realizes from inflation? The answer is that the debtor further benefits, and the reason is quite simple. While interest *receipts* are taxable, inter-est *payments* are deductible from income under current income tax laws and regulations. As interest rates increase under increasing inflation, the borrower is able to charge off a greater share of the interest costs as a deductible expense and borrow the funds for substantially less after the impacts of both inflation and tax bene-fits are accounted for.

Using the same illustration referred to above with regard to the lender, let us now examine the impact on the borrower under both inflation levels. Remember that under an inflationary envi-ronment, the borrower pays off the loan with cheaper dollars. For example, under a 2 percent inflation rate, the real cost of loan pay-ments declines by 2 percent each year since money with declining purchasing power is being used to repay the debt. The real cost of money to the borrower at a 5 percent interest rate would therefore be 3 percent after deducting the benefit received from inflation. Remember also that since interest payments are deductible expens-es by the borrower, taxable income is reduced by the amount of his or her interest payments, resulting in lower income tax payments. With this in mind, and assuming our borrower is in a 31 percent tax bracket, examine the two cases from the borrower's perspective:

	Case 1	Case 2
Interest rate paid on loan	5.0%	8.0%
Less tax benefit (31% bracket)	(1.6%)	(2.5%)
Less benefit due to inflation	(2.0%)	(5.0%)
After-tax real interest cost	1.4%	0.5%

The borrower's "real" interest cost, after adjustments are made for inflation and taxes, is therefore substantially reduced. In fact, the borrower gains from the inflation and tax impacts exactly what the lender loses, assuming both are in the same tax bracket. The message is therefore very clear. Current tax laws substantially amplify the tendency of inflation to redistribute wealth from creditors (or lenders) to debtors (or borrowers). The extent to which lenders are hurt and borrowers benefit depends upon both inflation rate and income tax bracket. This same rationale is used in Figure 2-1, which illustrates the extent of these impacts to both lenders and borrowers as a function of income tax bracket and for several different interest rates.

FIGURE 2–1

Real Gain and Cost
(After Tax and Assuming 3 Percent Inflation Rate

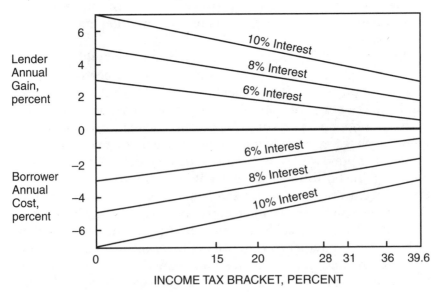

An annual inflation rate of 3 percent has been assumed. The situation becomes progressively worse for the creditor as the inflation rate increases. As indicated, the lender's loss in real gain is transferred to the borrower. It is apparent from these statistics that current tax provisions should strongly motivate individuals who anticipate a persistent inflation outlook to become debtors or borrowers. Under an inflationary environment, investors who become creditors by buying high-yield securities, such as corporate bonds yielding 8 or 9 percent interest annually, may find that they are earning much less on their investments than anticipated. The impact is even more unfavorable in the case of lower-yield investments such as Treasury bills, government bonds, savings accounts, life insurance programs, and similar "creditor"-type investment programs.

WINNERS AND LOSERS UNDER INFLATION

The redistribution of wealth among various elements of society results in both winners and losers under inflation. As indicated by the preceding discussion, such redistribution is from those who are predominately creditors to those who are predominately debtors. Since the accumulation of assets and the shift from a predominately debtor to creditor status is generally a function of age, the older segments of society tend to lose while the younger segments gain. It is quite natural and proper for young families to assume relatively large long-term debts. They have the prospect of many income-producing years before them. As people grow older, however, this prospect diminishes, and they therefore accumulate assets through various savings programs to provide the basis for a continued comfortable living standard as their income-producing capability declines and eventually terminates. Upon retirement, they have to depend on such assets to supplement other sources of company- or government-sponsored retirement income.

It is unfortunate that the element of society that is least able to afford the erosive power of inflation—the aged—is often hurt the most. Retired individuals, dependent upon fixed retirement incomes that were earned over a lifetime of work under the delusion that they would provide for a comfortable retirement, suddenly find their assets eroded and their incomes reduced in terms of anticipated real value or purchasing power. Regardless of age, however, the "loser" ranks include all those who have accumulated significant amounts of traditionally "safe," conservative, and non-speculative investments such as bonds, savings accounts, or insurance policies. This includes the large segment of preretirement-age middle-class America as well as those of retirement age.

Business firms can also be losers under inflation through over-stated profits. This is due to the fact that depreciation allowances are pegged to acquisition costs of facilities and equipment and sub-stantially understate replacement costs under an inflating econo-my. The result, of course, is that the understated depreciation allowances lead to overstated profits which are then taxed. Funds that should have been retained by the company for eventual use in financing replacement of facilities and equipment are lost in part to the government in taxes. The government, therefore, usually plays an extensive role in the redistribution process. Business firms may also benefit to the extent that they incur long-term debt which is ultimately paid off in cheaper dollars.

Individuals who are unable to accumulate significant assets might be expected to be relatively exempt from the impacts of inflation. Wages and prices tend to increase together during a wage-price spiral. The lead-lag relationship between the two depends upon whether cost-push or demand-pull pressures pre-dominate. Recipients of government-sponsored income distribu-tion programs—welfare, social security, unemployment compensation, etc.—are similarly not severely impacted, since pay-ments are adjusted periodically to compensate for inflationary changes. Those assets which low-income individuals are able to accumulate, however, are usually in the form of monetary savings which are eroded by inflation. The fact that very low income indi-viduals find it difficult to incur significant long-term debts such as mortgages (since their credit is usually not sufficiently good to qualify) means that they are unable to participate advantageously in the redistribution process brought about by inflation.

Inflation therefore tends to emphasize a redistribution of wealth from the old to the young, from those who have accumu-lated assets (other than the very wealthy) to the moderately low or middle income groups who are able to incur long-term debts and are in the early phases of building their estates. The very poor sit on the sidelines and generally do not participate to a significant degree. The very wealthy are able to avoid the redistribution impacts since they can afford to allocate a substantial portion of their estate to investments that keep pace with inflation—such as common stocks, real estate, and some of the other hedges. However, a very large segment of American society, those who have accumulated assets but are not wealthy, tend to retain their assets in more conservative forms of investment such as government bonds, life insurance, or savings accounts, all of which are eroded. The government gets a big take in the redistribution game and, in turn, plays a large role in subsequent secondary redistribution through government-sponsored programs. Inflation tends to escalate the government's role, not only because of the wealth redistribution requirements described above with the inherent burgeoning administrative implications, but also because of the demands upon government to increasingly intervene and control the economy and the inflation-related problems that arise. New bureaucracies are created and the cost of government itself is escalated. However, our intent is not to delve into these secondary impacts of inflation and the resultant governmental implications, but rather to provide an overview perspective to the problem and to call attention to the fact that a great segment of society is usually detrimentally impacted in terms of personal financial interests.

IN SUMMARY

Our purpose in this chapter has been to provide the reader with increased awareness to the implications of inflation. If you believe that persistent inflation is at least a moderate possibility for the future, then you must logically turn to those investment approaches which make you a borrower or a debtor. Investments that place you in the lender or creditor category expose you to the detrimental impacts of inflation described in the preceding discussion. In many respects, the successful investor is like a surf-rider. It is an impressive sight to watch these talented athletes skillfully mount the crest of a huge incoming wave and then cooperate with and harness the tremendous power of the sea to ride the wave gracefully to shore. The investor who selects the investment vehicle that is properly designed to meet the economic environment of the day will likely enjoy a smooth and profitable ride, though the environment itself may be quite turbulent. The wrong vehicle will carry its owner to crushing defeat. We believe real estate is one of those vehicles that provides the potential for a successful ride to financial security in this environment of modest inflation and even greater security in the event of greater inflationary turbulence in the days ahead.

CHAPTER 3

What You Need to Know about Profitability

You don't need to be a financial analyst to invest intelligently in real estate, but you must understand a few fundamentals that permit you to scope expected profitability. Before depositing money in a savings bank, most of us want to know the interest rate we will receive. Unfortunately, real estate buyers often invest without fully understanding how the expected appreciation in value of the property purchased can be translated into comparative or equivalent terms. This is because it is difficult to translate the projected cash flow of a typical real estate investment into an average annual interest rate or rate of return. Instead of an initial lump sum investment that yields a uniform stream of annual income, as in the case of savings accounts or bonds, real estate is more often purchased on an installment basis. While the cash flow may assume a variety of patterns, it typically involves a succession of annual net cash outflows and inflows until the property is sold several years later, at which time most of the net gain is received as a large, lump sum payment.

It is not readily apparent how such an irregular cash flow pattern can be expressed in the same simple terms used to describe the uniform annual earnings rate of fixed income investments. However, unless it is so expressed, it is very difficult to intelligently compare the relative appeal of real estate opportunities with alternative investment possibilities. Fortunately, this is possible.

But, unless you are familiar with the relatively complex analytical process required, it is somewhat difficult. Accordingly, graphs and charts are included in Chapters 5, 7, and 9 that provide rates of return for a wide range of scenarios. They translate basic information about the investment—information that should be at the disposal of the investor at the time of purchase—into an equivalent annual interest rate or rate of return. The rate thus identified represents a compound annual rate that may be compared meaningfully with the earnings rate of investments in savings accounts, bonds, or other fixed-income investments. These equivalent interest rates or rates of return are computed under methodology commonly referred to as the Internal Rate of Return or IRR. They take the time value of money into account and are realistic, conservative measures of profitability. The terms *internal rate of return, compound annual interest rate, return on invested capital,* and *return on investment* are used synonymously and interchangeably in ensuing discussion (although, strictly speaking, "return on investment" is not synonymous with IRR in accounting parlance).

It is appropriate at this point to call attention to the fact that various methods exist for computing rates of return with regard to real estate investments. Some are extremely misleading because they fail to take into consideration the time value of money. To illustrate, $1000 deposited in the bank at an annual interest rate of 10 percent will accumulate in value to $2594 by the end of 10 years if interest is not withdrawn. Note that the $1000 *does not* increase simply by $100 per year for 10 years, or by $1000, resulting in an accumulated value of $2000 at the end of 10 years. The reason the accumulated value is $2594 rather than $2000 is that interest is also earned on the accumulated gain each year, as well as on the original $1000 invested. This is called *compound interest.*

Promotional material by firms selling real estate or ownership shares in real estate ventures sometimes overstate the true potential rate of return by quoting an average annual interest rate that ignores this compounding effect. The preceding example helps illustrate this point. In this example, the $1000 invested for 10 years produced an accumulated value of $2594 at the end of that period, or a net gain of $1594 ($2594 minus $1000). The average annual gain is obviously one-tenth of this total gain, or $159 per year. It might, therefore, seem logical to state that the $159 gained each year on the $1000 original investment translates into a 15.9 percent annual rate of return, since $159 is 15.9 percent of $1000. However, the compound annual interest rate on this investment is actually only 10 percent, as stated earlier. This illustrates how statistics may be manipulated to produce a misleading profitability conclusion. Again, the reason for the misleading conclusion is that the interest rate in the example is not a compound annual interest rate, which is the more meaningful criterion, and one that may be compared appropriately with other investment opportunities. Stated another way, the erroneous solution fails to take into account the time value of money. Therefore, always demand or determine the projected *compound* annual rate of return for a contemplated real estate investment.

LEVERAGE

Leverage was mentioned earlier. Because of its importance, it merits further illustration. The basic principle is quite simple. A relatively small cash down payment is used to tie up or control property of substantial value. If the property inflates in value at a rate that exceeds the interest rate paid on the funds borrowed to finance the investment, a profitable outcome will be achieved. To illustrate, compare the profitability of a transaction involving property worth $100,000 purchased on a cash basis versus a leveraged basis. Assume the property is held for five years and that it doubles in value during that time. If the property is purchased on a cash basis for $100,000 and sold in five years for $200,000, it produces a gain of $100,000. This equates to a before tax gain of about 15 percent per year (compound annual interest) if we ignore selling costs and other expenses incurred in the transaction.

Now examine the return available from the same property purchased under a leveraged approach. Instead of purchasing the property for cash, assume that it is purchased on an installment basis with 20 percent or $20,000 down and the $80,000 balance subject to uniform annual payments at 9 percent interest over a 15-year period. Mortgage payment tables tell us that payments of $9738 per year will be required for this loan amount, interest rate, and time period. Again, assume that the property is sold in five years after doubling in value. The installment payments required during this period amount to $48,690 ($9738 per year times 5 years). At the time of resale, a balance of $64,080 still owed on the original loan must be repaid. The net gain from the $200,000 resale will be the amount left after deducting the sum of the cash outflows incurred during the five-year hold period:

Down Payment	$ 20,000
Installment Payments	48,690
Loan Balance After Five Years	64,080
Total Outflow	$132,770

A net gain of $67,230 is therefore realized ($200,000 minus $132,770).

Note that the net gain produced under the leveraged purchase is less than that achieved under the cash purchase ($67,230 versus $100,000). However, the cash purchase required an investment of $100,000 throughout the five-year period prior to resale, while the leveraged purchase required an initial cash outlay of only $20,000 (down payment) and an accumulated total of $68,690 after five years, or an average investment during this period of $44,345. Because of the relatively lower average investment level required under the leveraged purchase, the average annual rate of return equates to 22 percent, significantly higher than the 15 percent rate achieved under the cash purchase approach. The profitability or rate of return generated under the leveraged approach is therefore about one and one-half times that of the cash purchase.

Ways to Maximize Leverage

There are a variety of ways to maximize leverage. Leverage is increased by any means that defers or postpones cash outflow. This may be achieved by minimizing the down payment, extending the time period of the installment contract, and using deferred balloon payments in place of uniform periodic payments. The more aggressive investor can further increase leverage by borrowing the down payment or paying only the interest cost on the borrowed funds during the early years.

The disadvantage of leverage is that it carries increased risk. Examples of such risk are a temporary decline rather than increase in property value, or loss of employment, which could make it difficult to continue meeting installment payments. Although it is unlikely for most well-selected properties to decline in value over the long term, periods of depressed value can and do occur. Should the investor experience financial difficulties at such time and be unable to make the installment payments, it might become necessary to liquidate the property at a loss. The greater the leverage, the greater the potential rate of return, but also the greater the risk exposure. The amount of leverage used should therefore reflect the overall financial posture and the risk exposure that is appropriate for the individual involved.

Optimizing Leverage

An important objective concerning leverage is to avoid becoming a lender, whereby you would be *providing* leverage to the buyer at resale. The benefits realized by *obtaining* leverage in the purchase transaction will be largely nullified by providing leverage at the time of sale. An important key to maximizing profitability, therefore, is to borrow to buy, but to sell for cash if at all possible.

To illustrate, assume that land is purchased at 10 percent down with the balance to be paid off in uniform periodic payments over 10 years at 9 percent interest. Assume also that the property is sold after 3 years, during which time it appreciates in value at 20 percent per year. If the property is resold for cash (no leverage to the new buyer), an average rate of return of about 28 percent annually will be realized. If, instead, it is sold on an installment basis involving uniform annual payments at 9 percent interest over a 10-year period, the return realized will be significantly lower, with the extent of reduction depending on the down payment received. If the seller receives a 30 percent down payment at sale, the average annual rate of return would be about 17 percent. At a 15 percent down payment, the annual rate of return would drop to about 15 percent. These illustrations, incidentally, take into account representative buying and selling costs and are based on internal rate of return methodology.

An important strategy, therefore, is to select property that has the potential for resale on a cash basis. In the case of land, this means buying property that is relatively near the point of end-use application or the time that it will be developed in terms of some type of construction. The end-user must normally pay cash for land in order to receive clear title and proceed with development. In the case of rental houses, apartments, or other improved property, this strategy means avoiding installment contract terms at the time of sale. Let the buyer arrange for his own financing in order to cash you out if at all possible.

To summarize, here are some of the more important guidelines concerning profitability:

1. The average rate of return that the investment may be expected to yield can and should be estimated before you invest.

2. This rate should be based on computational methods that take the time value of money into account. More precisely, the internal rate of return method should be used. Do not be misled by profitability claims based upon simplistic and "rough approximation" approaches. Charts and guidelines in this book will help in this regard.

3. Use leverage in purchasing real estate in order to increase the profit rate earned on invested funds.

4. Avoid selling property on installment terms if at all possible. Select property for investment that provides the potential and expectation of resale under arrangements that cash you out after a reasonable hold period.

CHAPTER 4

Which Type of Real Estate?

Which type of real estate represents the best investment opportunity? The answer, of course, depends upon the unique circumstances and objectives of each investor and involves such considerations as the amount of cash available to invest, the income level desired, the magnitude of installment payments that can be comfortably handled, tax shelter objectives, the level of risk that is acceptable, and whether the primary objective is income or growth.

Land, rental houses, and apartments provide a broad spectrum of real estate opportunities that meet the varied needs and interests of most investors. One does not have to look very far to locate such investment opportunities, and the average individual already possesses much of the knowledge important to making good selections. Most of us are knowledgeable about the neighborhoods in and the areas surrounding the city or town in which we live—knowledgeable about prevailing real estate prices, areas representing the greatest growth potential, and areas to be avoided because of undesirable features or trends. Moreover, the level of capital required for these three types of real estate investment is within an acceptable range for most middle-income investors, making investment through group or syndicated arrangements unnecessary. Limited partnerships, joint ventures, partnerships, and real estate investment trusts all have their place and offer some appealing features, but they do not permit the investor to control the investment or to tailor it to his or her own circumstances. (Group investments are discussed more fully in Chapter 11.)

The best type of real estate investment depends upon the individual's unique circumstances and investment objectives or "financial profile." Subsequent chapters describe typical cash flow and profitability profiles for land, rental houses and apartments, highlight the pertinent investment differences between each, and provide guidelines for selecting good opportunities and scoping profit potential. Emphasis is placed upon the financial assessment since profit is the underlying purpose and motivation of any investment.

YOUR FINANCIAL PROFILE

Financial profile can be broadly defined in terms of two basic factors: *cash position* and *income position*. Cash position refers to the amount of capital or cash available to invest or to which the investor has access. Some properties require relatively large down payments, while others do not. Income position refers to current and future earning power or income level and the extent to which the investor is financially postured to support or "feed" investments that require installment payments.

Figure 4-1 illustrates four basic financial profiles or combinations of cash and income positions:

Profile 1.   Weak cash and income positions
Profile 2.   Strong cash position but weak income position
Profile 3.   Weak cash position but strong income position
Profile 4.   Strong cash and income positions

Gradations obviously exist among these four profiles. For example, many individuals might more accurately be described as having moderate rather than strong or weak cash and income positions. Nevertheless, the four extremes provide a useful spectrum for describing the relative merits of various types of real estate for people with distinct financial profiles.

In Figure 4-2, the matrix has been expanded to describe the important investment objectives or characteristics applicable to each profile and to indicate the extent that each type of real estate—land, rental houses, and apartments—best satisfies the objectives of each.

FIGURE 4–1

Financial Profile Matrix

		CASH POSITION	
		WEAK	STRONG
INCOME POSITION	WEAK	Financial Profile 1	Financial Profile 2
	STRONG	Financial Profile 3	Financial Profile 4

Individuals who fall under Financial Profile 1—persons with little money in the bank and a salary that leaves little or no residual income for investment—should probably not invest. Rather, such individuals should wait until their income level increases sufficiently or until they accumulate an investment nest egg.

Financial Profile 2 involves individuals in a strong cash but weak income position. This profile consists of those who have accumulated significant assets that can be readily converted to cash—savings accounts, stocks, or bonds—but who have relatively low income from other sources. This typically describes older individuals who have accumulated savings but are retired or no longer in their prime earning years. The principal investment thrust for this profile is toward income-producing investments or those requiring low carrying costs; growth is a secondary objective. Apartment houses meet these requirements quite well. Rental houses produce rental income, but the net cash flow during the hold period may be negative because of taxes, insurance, mortgage payments, and other expenses.

FIGURE 4–2

Typical Investment Objectives for Each Financial Profile

		CASH POSITION		
		WEAK	**STRONG**	
INCOME POSITION	**WEAK**	Profile 1 Don't Invest!	Profile 2 • Minimal Carrying Cost (A) • Income Producing (A) • Cash Discount or Assumption Opportunities (A, L, R)	Apartment Houses or Other Strong Income Property
	STRONG	Profile 3 • Maximum Tax Shelter Benefits (A, R) • Deferred Gain and Future Cash-Out (L, R) • Maximum Leverage (L)	Profile 4 • Maximum Tax Shelter Benefits (R, A) • Deferred Gain and Future Cash-Out (L, R) • Cash Discount or Assumption Opportunities (A, L, R) • Maximum Leverage (L)	Land or Rental Houses or Apartments—All Are Good!

Land or Rental Houses

Suitability Code:
(L) = Best suited by land
(R) = Best suited by rental houses
(A) = Best suited by apartments

Another investment strategy for individuals in Financial Profile 2 might involve price discount opportunities available through cash purchases or substantial down payments. This is particularly applicable to land investments involving installment contracts in which the seller and buyer enter into a contractual agreement based upon mutually acceptable terms. This instrument is quite common in land sales since the financing of unimproved property is usually unavailable through conventional lending institutions. Since sellers generally prefer to be cashed out as early as possible, it is usually possible to negotiate a reduction in total price in exchange for a large down payment and/or a relatively short contract period. Similar opportunities exist for rental houses and apartments, but less frequently than for land since the buyer of improved property usually obtains financing from a conventional lending source rather than from the seller, thereby permitting the seller to be cashed out.

As indicated in Figure 4-2, apartment houses are somewhat more responsive than either land or rental houses to the investment objectives of persons falling into Financial Profile 2.

Financial Profile 3 is composed of individuals with relatively high income levels but limited cash or savings. This typically describes younger and middle-age individuals who are in their high or increasing income years of life but have not yet accumulated significant savings. This group typically seeks opportunities that defer or minimize tax exposure. In addition, high leverage opportunities are appropriate since high and growing income levels provide the capability to carry loan payments. As noted in Figure 4-2, this profile is best accommodated by rental houses and land investments. Although apartments and rental houses are both appealing tax shelters, apartments usually produce a net positive income during the hold period, while rental houses often operate at a negative cash flow until sold. Rental houses are therefore oriented toward deferred gain, while apartments produce gain partially on a current basis (rental income) and partially on a deferred basis. Maximum leverage opportunities are best accommodated by land, where typical down payments may range from 10 to 30 percent or lower. Apartments and rental houses require higher down payments on the average and also afford fewer opportunities for deferred or balloon payments and other approaches that maximize leverage. In general, land and rental houses appear to be the best bets for those in Financial Profile 3.

The remaining group, Financial Profile 4, is composed of those fortunate few who enjoy both strong cash and income positions. Land, rental houses, and apartments all represent opportunities for this group. The most appropriate type of real estate for those with this profile is therefore determined on the basis of individual circumstances or by factors other than those describing the financial profile.

OTHER FACTORS

Several other factors impacting on the type of real estate to invest in are relative liquidity, the amount of time and personal involvement required in managing the investment, the extent to which government regulations make life more complex, and the extent to which it is possible to influence growth in value through improvement or upgrading. Figure 4-3 summarizes the relative merits of land, rental houses, and apartments in relation to these considerations.

Rental houses offer the advantage of relatively good liquidity since a broad base of prospective home buyers is almost always available, generally permitting sale within a relatively short time

FIGURE 4–3

Other Factors Influencing Type of Real Estate

● BEST

● NEXT BEST

Factor	Type of Real Estate		
	Land	Rental Houses	Apartments
Quick Liquidity		●	●
Minimal Management or Personal Involvement	●	●	(Depends on Size and Management Arrangement)
Least Subject to Governmental Regulation or Interference	● (Environmental Regulations)	●	● (Rent Controls, Tenant Rights, etc.)
Re-Zone or Use-Upgrade Opportunities	●	●	

frame. Apartments are somewhat more difficult to sell because they involve a different market. They are sold to investors rather than to consumers, and there are fewer investors than consumers. Land is the least desirable in terms of liquidity, since it should be sold to an end-user rather than to another speculator in order to maximize profitability. The end-user who finds the land well suited to his or her needs will usually pay a premium price and must normally cash out the seller in order to obtain title and proceed with development. Speculators tend to press for bargain prices and highly leveraged terms, which diminish the profit potential to the seller. As a result, it is much more difficult to find a good buyer for land in a very short period of time.

Land is most appealing in terms of time and management demands during the hold period. Rental houses require a relatively high level of attention since the investor must perform or oversee such functions as renter selection, rent collection, cleanup and preparation between occupancies, and maintenance and repair work. Apartment houses impose similar demands unless there are enough units to justify a manager, in which case the investor's personal involvement in day-to-day problems is greatly diminished.

Governmental regulations are always a concern. Rental houses do not currently present many problems in this regard. Apartment housing is more vulnerable to tenant rights legislation and public agitation during periods of housing shortage to restrict owner prerogatives concerning tenant selection, evictions, condominium conversion, and other actions that might be viewed as contrary to the public interest. Governmental intervention with respect to land is primarily in the areas of increasing regulations related to environmental protection and land use.

Another factor to be considered is the potential for value building through investor initiatives. Land provides significant opportunities in this regard through rezoning, subdivision, and clearing to enhance visibility and appeal. Opportunities with respect to rental houses and apartments are largely in the area of building improvements. For example, properties that are rundown but basically sound can be enhanced through superficial repairs and relatively inexpensive improvements. Depending upon one's time, skills, abilities, and interests, therefore, opportunities exist for value building in land, rental houses, and apartments.

In summary, different types of real estate suit different needs. One type is not superior to another as an investment vehicle except as viewed in relation to the financial circumstances, talents, and interests of each individual. This is why it's necessary to understand your own orientation before pursuing real estate investment.

The next five chapters deal more specifically with each of these three types of real estate investment: rental houses, apartments, and land.

CHAPTER 5

Rental Houses

Rental houses offer one of the best opportunities to both first-time and experienced real estate investors. Good buys are not difficult to identify, and rental houses offer significant tax benefits. Several factors are important in determining good rental house investments—those offering the potential for a favorable rate of return. Appreciation rate is probably the single most important factor and is a function of how good a buy is negotiated at the time of purchase and how rapidly the property increases in value. Accordingly, you can directly influence a favorable appreciation rate by careful selection and by buying houses at below market value, while selling them at market value. Beyond this, the key is to select houses in areas where future demand will be high. Figure 5-1 illustrates the sensitivity of profitability to appreciation rate for a typical rental house investment. The assumptions for the investment scenario are summarized on the chart, and several curves are included for different levels of rental income. Note that the rate of return increases quite dramatically as the appreciation rate increases.

As might be expected, rental income is the other primary factor in profitability outcome. Figure 5-2 illustrates how profitability improves for a representative investment scenario as the monthly rental income, expressed as a percentage of purchase price, increases. Again, the assumptions for the scenario are summarized on the chart.

FIGURE 5-1

Rental Houses: Impact of Appreciation Rate on Profitability

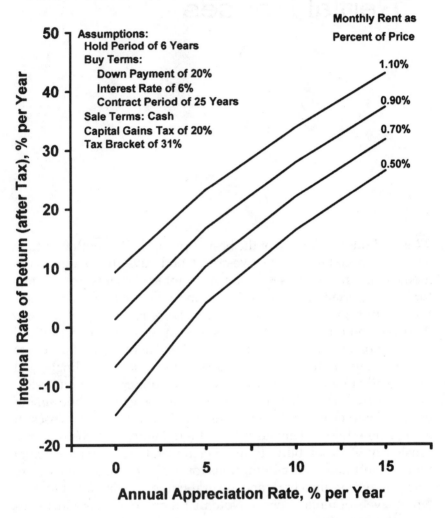

Rental income and appreciation rates tend to go hand in hand since rental levels bear a close relationship to housing values and demand. If housing sales are stagnant and values are not appreciating as fast or faster than inflation, it is probably due to a surplus of available housing, a condition that tends to depress rents, as well. In purchasing rental houses, it is important to select those for

FIGURE 5–2

Rental Houses: Impact of Rental Income on Profitability

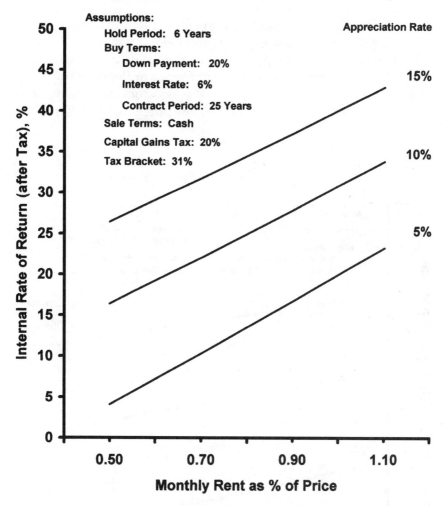

which intermediate term prospects—say, the next five years or so—
are favorable for good rates of growth in value. This normally
requires that the basic economic conditions of the area are strong.
If the area is undergoing industrial expansion with the influx of
new companies and corresponding employment growth, it is a
good bet that demand for housing will be strong in the future and
that housing values will appreciate at a healthy pace. On the other

hand, if the area is economically stable, stagnant, or depressed, the prospects for good appreciation rates, as well as favorable rental levels, are probably poor.

The third key to achieving a favorable rate of return in rental house investments is down payment. Down payment determines the extent to which leverage is used and, as already discussed and illustrated in Chapter 3, is a major influence in financial outcome. Moreover, down payment is a factor the investor can actively influence through negotiations at the time of purchase. In general, the

FIGURE 5-3

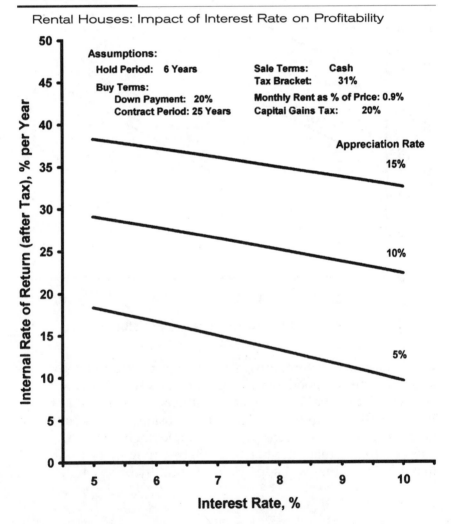

Rental Houses: Impact of Interest Rate on Profitability

lower the down payment, the better. Twenty percent down is common, but in many instances lower down payments are negotiable.

Finally, the interest rate under the purchase contract is also a factor that influences profitability, but is much less critical than the other factors discussed. Figure 5-3 illustrates the sensitivity of profitability to interest rate for a representative rental house investment scenario.

CASH FLOW PATTERNS

In considering rental house investments, it is necessary to be prepared for the possibility of a negative cash flow during all or part of the hold period. To put it another way, unless the down payment is relatively high, the monthly rental income may not be sufficient to cover the monthly cash outflow for such items as mortgage payments, taxes, insurance, and maintenance expenses. Moreover, since one of the strategies may be to maximize leverage by minimizing down payment, a negative cash flow is not unusual.

A representative cash flow pattern for a favorable rental house investment is illustrated in Figure 5-4.

This shows the net annual cash flow (after tax)—the net amount that will either be received or expended each year for a rental house purchased for $100,000. Other key assumptions are summarized on the chart. Note that a favorable ratio of monthly rent to price, 0.8 percent, has been assumed. As indicated, the investor in this example incurs a rather large cash outflow of $22,000 at the outset due to the down payment and closing costs incurred at the time of purchase. The after-tax net cash flow turns slightly positive in the second year and gradually increases for each successive year, reaching about $4400 at the ninth year. A large net cash inflow of $145,400 occurs at the tenth year, when the house is sold. This cash inflow at the tenth year consists of the net receipts from the sale of the house after paying the balance owed on the mortgage, selling costs, and other expenses. This is representative for a house in this price and rental range. Had the ratio of monthly rent to price been only 0.4 percent, however, instead of the 0.8 percent illustrated, a negative cash flow of about $3000 a year would have prevailed until the sale.

Figure 5-5 is the same example presented in terms of *cumulative* cash flow.

It is simply the cumulative investment year by year through the life of the investment. As noted, the cash flow on a cumulative

F I G U R E   5–4

Net Annual Cash Flow After Tax, Typical Rental House
Investment

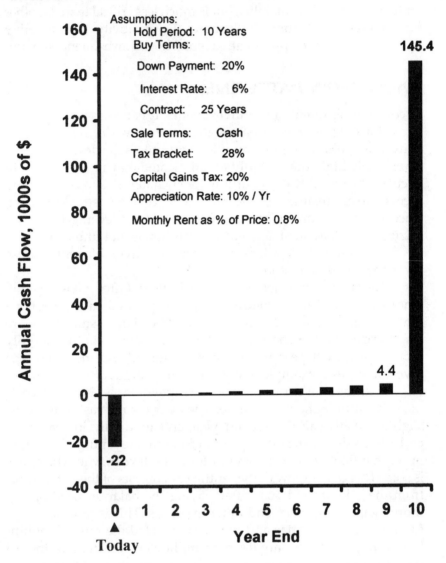

FIGURE 5–5

Rental House Cumulative Net Cash Flow after Tax

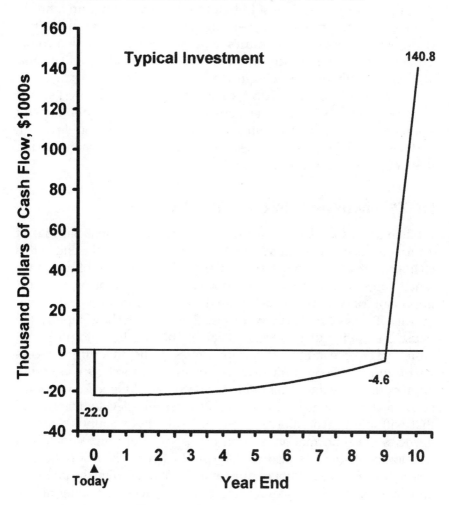

basis remains negative, although gradually improving, through the ninth year. Upon sale at the tenth year, the net cumulative gain is $140,800. The after-tax annual rate of return for this example is about 24 percent. Again, if the ratio of monthly rent to price is dropped to 0.4 percent instead of the 0.8 percent illustrated, the negative cash flow would grow to over $51,500 by the ninth year, and the net cumulative gain would drop about 39 percent. The rate of return would be cut almost in half. The basic message is: Expect to wait until the house is sold before realizing a net gain, and, in some cases, be prepared to feed the investment until such time. Although inflationary pressures tend to escalate rental income, expenses (taxes, insurance, and maintenance) will also escalate and at least partially offset such growth in income.

In view of this cash flow pattern, rental houses are best suited to investors who have other sources of income, do not depend upon the investment as a source of income during the hold period, and have sufficient financial reserves to feed the investment during this period, should it become necessary.

DETERMINING PROFITABILITY

Profitability, as explained earlier, is defined as the internal rate of return produced by the investment. A series of charts at the end of this chapter enables you to determine the approximate rate of return for rental house investments based upon several key variables, the most important of which are anticipated appreciation rate and rental income. To use the charts, you must first estimate how rapidly the house is expected to appreciate in value. This will be a judgment call based on the prevailing appreciation rates in the area during recent years, and based on an assessment of future prospects concerning appreciation in value. Real estate firms are usually good sources for such data, as well as for information concerning development plans that will affect area values. A visit to local city or county planning agencies for information concerning population projections and development plans is also usually productive. It is worthwhile to research several recent house sales in order to determine the purchase and subsequent sale prices and the resulting average annual rate of appreciation represented by these transactions. To compute appreciation rate, three items of information are needed in this research: purchase price, sale price, and the number of years that have elapsed from purchase to sale for houses comparable to the one you are considering for purchase. Figure 5-6 can then be used to translate this information into the average annual appreciation rate of the properties.

To use this chart, first determine the increase factor. This is simply the sale price divided by the purchase price. For example, if

FIGURE 5-6

Increase Factors

		Hold Period in Years								
		1	2	3	4	5	6	7	8	9	10
Percent Annual Appreciation	5	1.05	1.10	1.16	1.22	1.28	1.34	1.41	1.48	1.55	1.63
	10	1.10	1.21	1.33	1.46	1.61	1.77	1.95	2.14	2.36	2.59
	15	1.15	1.32	1.52	1.75	2.01	2.31	2.66	3.06	3.52	4.05
	20	1.20	1.44	1.73	2.07	2.49	2.99	3.58	4.30	5.16	6.19
	25	1.25	1.56	1.95	2.44	3.05	3.81	4.77	5.96	7.45	9.31
	30	1.30	1.69	2.20	2.86	3.71	4.83	6.27	8.16	10.6	13.8
	35	1.35	1.82	2.46	3.32	4.48	6.05	8.17	11.0	14.9	20.1
	40	1.40	1.96	2.74	3.84	5.38	7.53	10.5	14.8	20.7	28.9
	45	1.45	2.10	3.05	4.42	6.41	9.29	13.5	19.5	28.3	41.1
	50	1.50	2.25	3.38	5.06	7.59	11.4	17.1	25.6	38.4	57.7

the property was purchased five years ago for $50,000 and sold recently for $100,000, the increase factor is $100,000 divided by $50,000, or 2. Stated another way, the property doubled in value over a five-year period. To translate this into the average annual appreciation rate, refer to Figure 5-6, locate the number that is closest to the increase factor of 2 for the five-year hold period, and read off the corresponding appreciation rate. The factor of 2.01 under column 5 is the closest factor in this case and corresponds to an annual appreciation rate of 15 percent.

The second important item of information needed in order to use the profitability analysis charts at the end of this chapter is the monthly rental income the house will produce at the time of purchase. If the house is currently rented, you will, of course, have this information. Otherwise, it will be necessary to estimate the monthly rent. The classified advertisement section of local newspapers will provide the going rental rates for comparable dwellings. In the profitability analysis charts, the monthly rental income is expressed as a percent of the purchase price. For example, if the house sells for $100,000 and can be rented for $800 per month, the monthly rent may be expressed as a percent of the price simply by dividing the monthly rent by the price and multiplying by 100:

$$\text{Monthly rent as percent of price} = \frac{\$800}{\$100,000} \times 100 = 0.8\%$$

Figure 5-7 illustrates use of the profitability analysis charts, using this example in which the monthly rent is 0.8 percent of the price. Also assume that your analysis concludes that the house is likely to appreciate in value at about 10 percent per year over the next five years, after which you intend to sell it. As can be seen, the average annual return on investment (or internal rate of return) that may be realistically anticipated is about 23 percent. Note also that the rate of return thus determined is on an after-tax basis for an investor in the 28 percent tax bracket. Other assumptions are as indicated on the chart.

In using the profitability charts, select the one that most closely approximates your tax bracket, the expected hold period, and the current interest rate. The hold period is the number of years the house is expected to be retained before sale. The interest rate is that of the mortgage or installment contract under which the house is purchased. Since the charts cover only selected values for these factors, you may have to refer to more than one chart and do some interpolation if the actual values differ from the conditions covered.

It is emphasized that the rates of return provided by these charts are intended as general guidelines and are predicated upon a number of representative assumptions. A 20 percent down payment is assumed at purchase, along with representative values for taxes, maintenance costs, selling expenses, and escalation rates applicable to such costs, expenses, and rental income over time. The specific assumptions are summarized immediately following the charts section. Although representative values have been used in developing the charts, it must be recognized that actual values may differ somewhat. For example, the house may be purchased under either a larger or smaller down payment than the 20 percent assumed. Nevertheless, the charts provide a good approximation of expected profitability for various combinations of purchase price, rental income, appreciation rate, and interest rate. You should find them extremely helpful as a *preliminary screening tool* to

FIGURE 5-7

Rental Houses

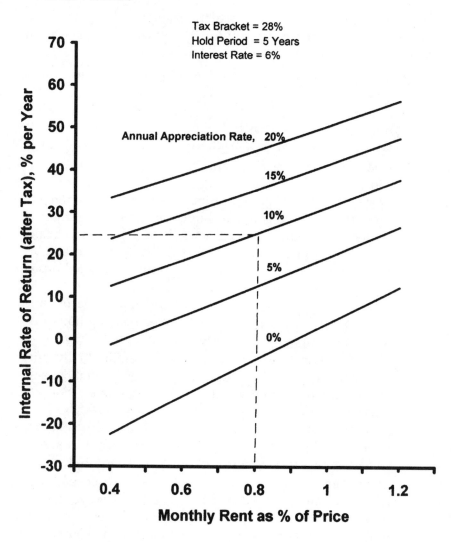

test the acceptability of prospective rental house investments in terms of potential profitability. However, you should follow up with a more precise and customized analysis, using actual data in place of the general assumptions reflected in the charts, before making a final decision concerning the investment.

ADVANTAGES AND DISADVANTAGES TO BUYING SINGLE FAMILY HOMES

There are several advantages to buying single family homes as investment property, particularly for those just getting started in real estate investing. These include:

- ◆ It takes much less money to buy a house than to buy an apartment building or other commercial property. Accordingly, the risk is lower in the event that things do not work out as expected.

- ◆ Houses offer much better liquidity than do other types of income property or even land. Most home buyers are consumers, rather than investors, and there are many more consumers than investors. Apartments, commercial property, and land can take a long time to sell. But there is always a ready market for homes that are offered at a fair price, except in areas that are economically depressed. Prudent investors do not normally purchase rental houses in economically depressed areas unless there is information that some event will bring about an economic turnaround for the region, in which case buying houses at depressed prices might represent a real opportunity.

- ◆ The single family house investor has the ability to diversify in terms of location. The purchase of several rental houses in different locations diversifies the risk of one location proving undesirable in terms of resale. In contrast, purchasing an apartment with a number of units could be financially devastating if a mistake in judgment is made concerning location in terms of rentability and resale.

- ◆ The owner of a few single family houses can act as his or her own manager if inclined to do so. The do-it-yourself owner can also take care of minor repairs, screen potential renters personally, and take care of the record keeping, thereby minimizing overhead costs to maintain the property. Professional management becomes much more necessary in multiple family housing.

There are also disadvantages to investing in single family houses, as opposed to other types of real estate:

- Managing several rental houses can be either more time consuming or more expensive than managing an apartment building where all of the units are in one location. It may be economically feasible to have a resident manager in an apartment complex, whereas single family homes are usually managed by the owner, although retaining a management firm is an option. If the management function is contracted out to a real estate management firm, the per house management fee will likely be much greater than the per unit management cost for an apartment complex. In this regard, single family houses are much less desirable than land investments, which do not require such management.

- The cost of repairs can be relatively high for single family houses. For example, if you need to reroof the house, the cost would be relatively high on a per unit basis compared to an apartment complex. Although it would cost more to reroof an apartment building, the cost is spread over the number of rental units in the building.

- When the tenant vacates a single family house, the rental income ceases entirely until it is rerented. It is either 100 percent occupied or 100 percent vacant. Owners of apartment houses typically take into account a certain vacancy allowance and therefore do not experience the same abrupt cash flow fluctuations caused by vacancies.

- Renters of single family houses tend to be more unstable than apartment renters. People renting single family houses are often between moves after selling their own home, or are planning to buy their own home in the future as soon as they can afford to do so. Apartment renters, on the other hand, tend to be more committed to the rental approach as opposed to home ownership.

FIXER-UPPER STRATEGIES

Fixer-upper strategies can apply to both apartments as well as single family houses, but it is particularly well suited to the latter. It can be particularly appealing to those who like to work with their hands and are in a position to live in the house during the fix-up process. Good fixers, in such cases, are properties that are basically sound but that need a lot of superficial or cosmetic upgrade—paint, refinishing, minor structural improvements, and landscape work. These activities do not usually involve large cash outlays but do require time and effort. The investor can fix up the house at his or her own pace while living in it, increase its rental and sale value, and realize the benefits of more favorable bank financing terms available by virtue of an owner-occupied purchase. When the renovation work is complete and another rental house investment opportunity is identified, the house is rented or sold and the investor moves on to the next house to repeat the cycle. This scenario is obviously not for everyone. It involves moving and disruption to the family, and it may be impractical if the house currently occupied is not suitable as a rental property. It remains a possibility, nevertheless, for those who are mobile and enjoy fixers as a value-building technique.

Regardless of whether the above approach is involved, the purchase of fixer-upper properties should be evaluated using the following steps:

1. Determine what the value of the property will be after it is repaired and brought up to the condition required to make it comparable to other houses in the area in terms of size and quality. In other words, determine what the value of the house will be on the market after you have completed the necessary repairs to upgrade it to the condition of comparable houses in the neighborhood.

2. Determine the cost of repairs to accomplish this. This involves making an itemized list and getting cost estimates of required repairs. It may involve getting supplier or subcontractor bids or estimates for major repairs such as window replacement, roof replacement, painting, etc. Even if you intend to do all or much of the work yourself, the cost of repairs should reflect what you would pay to have others do the work. If you do the work, part of what you must recover upon resale is the value of your labor.

3. Estimate the cost you will incur to sell the property after the repairs are completed, as well as the holding cost

(interest payments on the mortgage) during the time period from the date that it is purchased until it is sold or available to rent. For example, if this hold period is about three months and the house costs $150,000, your interest costs on these funds for that period of time might be about 2 percent (one-fourth of the annual rate of 8 percent). It will likely cost about 9 to 10 percent of the resale value to cover real estate commissions and closing costs, and you will likely incur costs of about 2 percent of the purchase price at the time of purchase. These overhead expenses aggregate to about 14 percent. If the house is held longer or if the interest rate on the mortgage at purchase is higher than 8 percent, the overhead cost will be higher. A reasonable average overhead cost to use is therefore about 15 percent.

4. With all of the above information at hand, you can now compute the price that you should pay for the fixer-upper property under consideration. If you plan to sell the house immediately after it is fixed up, the buy price should be the estimated resale price (item 1, above), less the estimated repair cost (item 2), less the overhead cost (item 3), less the profit you expect to realize. A good minimum profit or gain should be 15 to 20 percent of the selling price.

To illustrate this process, assume the fixer-upper you are interested in buying will sell for about $150,000 after you have fixed it up. Assume also that it will cost an estimated $10,000 in repairs to bring it up to acceptable condition. The amount that you can afford to offer for this property is calculated as follows:

Resale price:	$150,000
Less:	
Repair Cost:	($10,000)
Overhead Cost:	
(15% × $150,000)	($22,500)
Profit:	
(15% × $150,000)	($22,500)
Purchase Price:	$95,000

If you can't purchase the property for $95,000, it will not provide a gain to you that makes good financial sense under a buy, fix-up, and resell scenario. If, on the other hand, your plan is to purchase the property, fix it up, and then rent it for the next few years, the profit included in the above calculation can be eliminated. Under a buy, fix-up, and rent scenario, a price of $117,500 would be justified ($95,000 + $22,500) since you are purchasing the property for rental, rather than a quick turnaround resale. Since the profit will be based on rental income and appreciation in value over a number of years, the immediate profit required under the first scenario does not apply.

SELECTING THE HOUSE

Good rental properties are frequently overlooked by potential purchasers who evaluate houses in terms of personal likes and dislikes rather than from an objective investment perspective. It doesn't matter if the house has only 900 square feet, two bedrooms, and a single bath, provided it will rent easily and appreciate in value at a good rate. Patience is important. Don't be discouraged if you look at a number of houses and none of them seem to make good investment sense. You may look at 20 or more houses over a two month period and find nothing suitable, and then all at once locate several attractive opportunities. Get a good real estate agent to look for you, but also follow up on "For Sale by Owner" ads in your local newspaper or on the Internet (see Chapter 12). Locating good rental houses requires significant time spent looking over prospective opportunities. There is no way to bypass this requirement.

In seeking attractive opportunities, here are general criteria to keep in mind:

Good Neighborhood. Some neighborhoods go through cycles that include a deterioration phase. It is important to select houses in neighborhoods that are either still developing and on the upswing or that are relatively stable. Neighborhood deterioration is not necessarily a function of age. Many neighborhoods are quite old but very stable, and the properties show evidence of good maintenance and care. Some relatively new neighborhoods, on the other hand, such as inexpensive tract-home developments, begin to deteriorate at a relatively early age. This doesn't mean that you are limited to only the most desirable neighborhoods. Houses may be so overpriced in extremely popular neighborhoods that appreciation rates will be lower than in good but perhaps less exclusive or less popular areas. Always look over neighborhoods with an eye toward what they will be like in about five years, when you will probably want to sell the house.

Location. Look for good locations within good neighborhoods. From a sale standpoint, it is a good idea to avoid property adjacent to freeways, shopping centers, multistory buildings, or schools. From a rental standpoint, properties should not be too remote from major shopping areas and should have good access to major arterials and public transportation systems. It is also a good idea to select property that is reasonably convenient to your own home or place of business. This simplifies things considerably when you need to make repairs, clean up after tenants depart, and interview or show the property to prospective new tenants.

Condition. The property purchased should be in good condition and free from the prospects of major repairs or renovation, unless the "move-in-and-fix-up" approach appeals to you. Assuming it does not, the house should be clean, freshly painted, in good repair, with a relatively new roof, well landscaped, and preferably no more than 20 or 25 years old. A home in this condition will be immediately rentable, will minimize additional near-term cash outlays for repairs, and will attract desirable tenants—those who are likely to be reliable, take good care of the property, and pay top rental rates. Relatively new roofs are important because they are a big expense. A house that is more than 25 years old is often a candidate for plumbing, wiring, or heating system repairs, all of which can be quite costly. Generally, the newer the home, the better. Although some older homes have exceptionally sturdy construction features, the risk of costly repairs is also greater. Look for owner-occupied houses with evidence of good maintenance and care. Avoid homes that have outmoded heating systems, and those without garages.

Price. The primary constraint on price is its relationship to rental income and appreciation rate. The more favorable rent-to-price relationships generally occur in the lower price ranges. Rental income increases with the value of the house, but not proportionately, as illustrated in Figure 5-8.

As indicated, rental rates climb rather steeply along with the value of the house at the lower end of the price scale, but tend to level off at the higher end. This is because beyond a certain rental level, people tend to seek alternatives to renting, such as purchasing their own house, con-

FIGURE 5–8

Relationship of Rent Potential versus Property Value

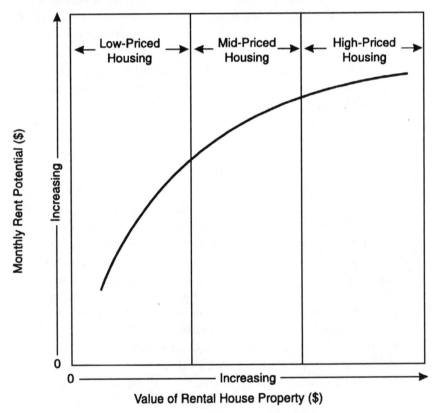

dominium, or town house. For this reason, rental houses in the low-to-moderate price range usually make the best investments. In terms of surrounding area values, it is generally wise to buy a house in the low-to-middle price range of the community. A house that is below the community average value tends to benefit by the more-expensive surrounding homes and will probably be relatively easy to sell. Most people are reluctant, on the other hand, to purchase a home that is in the upper price range relative to surrounding area values.

Size. Three- or four-bedroom properties offer the advantage of a wider resale market. Apart from this, there is no real advantage over a two-bedroom home. In fact, smaller homes may offer a more favorable rent-to-price ratio.

Extras. There are a variety of other factors that enhance the value of the property and influence the ease with which it is ultimately sold. An attractively sized and shaped lot, appealing landscaping, fireplaces, insulated walls and windows, a double garage, built-in appliances, and similar features are all desirable extras. However, they are not essential and need not be included, provided the price is consistent with the overall value. Other special features, such as air-conditioning in warmer climates or basements in other parts of the country, may be important. The important principle is that special features important to specific communities or regions should be included if they are generally expected by either the prospective tenants or future buyers.

Contract Terms. After locating a house that offers good profit potential and satisfies other selection criteria, an offer is made and the negotiation process begins. (Negotiating principles and tactics are discussed in Chapter 10.) Assuming that basic agreement has been reached between the buyer and seller, a contract usually referred to as an earnest money receipt, deposit receipt, or real estate agreement is drawn up. This is an agreement in which a sum of money or deposit is provided by the buyer to bind the offer. The deposit is applied to the down payment in the purchase transaction, provided the conditions of the agreement are fulfilled and the sale takes place. If not, the deposit is refunded to the would-be buyer.

This arrangement is fair since the seller must take the house off the market if he or she accepts the offer and should be protected from loss in the event the buyer backs out of the deal for reasons other than those permitted by the agreement. Should the buyer arbitrarily withdraw from the transaction, he or she would normally forfeit this deposit. The agreement is signed by the buyer and then presented to the seller for their signature. In most states, the offer is binding as soon as the seller accepts.

The deposit is usually placed in a trustee account of the real estate firm handling the transaction or that of the title company. The deposit should not be given directly to the seller, but placed with a title company in escrow. In the event that the seller does not like the terms of the agreement, they may write in the desired changes on the contract in ink, initial the changes, sign the agreement thus revised, and return the contract to the buyer for concurrence. If the buyer accepts these revisions, he or she also initials each change, and the agreement is thus consummated. If the buyer finds the changes unacceptable and does not initial them, he is no longer bound by the terms of the contract and may withdraw from the transaction. Since this contract legally commits the buyer to a rather substantial transaction, it is important that it be carefully reviewed for completeness, including all special conditions or terms necessary to make the transaction acceptable. Although preprinted forms are generally used, adequate space is provided to write or type in additional conditions or terms. In all cases, consult an attorney before signing the papers.

Here are some typical items that should be covered by the contract:

- ◆ A complete description of the property, including legal description of the boundaries, address, and items other than real estate to be included in the sale, such as draperies, furniture, appliances, etc.

- Repairs or improvements to be made to the house or property by the seller prior to closing.
- Amount of deposit.
- Financing terms. Real estate brokers or salespersons sometimes pass over this point lightly, assuring you that satisfactory financing can be arranged. Don't take a chance. If financing is unavailable, you could forfeit the deposit unless the terms of the contract make your acquisition of satisfactory financing a necessary condition. It is therefore essential that the financing terms be specified with respect to loan amount, interest rate, loan period, and type of loan.
- Inspections. In certain parts of the country, it is wise to include the requirement for a termite and foundation inspection, along with the provision that the seller pay for any corrective work deemed necessary by such inspection. Alternatively, there can be an escape clause if the house fails to pass the inspection. You may also specify other inspections to be made and make the sale contingent upon satisfactory results or approvals by the parties performing such inspections. It is also desirable to specify that the selection of inspectors or inspection firms will be made by the buyer, thereby ensuring that qualified parties are selected who represent your interests.
- Time limitation. Specify the date by which the offer must be accepted and after which it becomes null and void and the deposit must be refunded.
- Warranties. Be sure the contract form provides for some type of property warranty clause. This is a statement that warrants that all grounds and improvements will be maintained in their present condition and delivered in such condition at the close of escrow. It is also desirable to include a statement providing for the buyer's right to inspect the premises prior to closing and requiring the seller to pay for any repairs that may be necessary with respect to the warranty provision.
- Title Insurance. The contract should provide for a title insurance policy in the amount of the purchase price that

protects the buyer from potential loss due to possible error or omission in examining the title or against other possible defects against a clear title. In the event the title is not insurable, terms should specify that the buyer is released from the contract obligations and entitled to a refund of the deposit.

SELLING OR REFINANCING THE PROPERTY

After five years or so you may want to sell the rental house. The primary motivation for selling is to extract the equity that has been building up due to the appreciation in value and because of the reduction in the loan balance through mortgage or loan payments. Most of the equity buildup will be attributable to appreciation in value, since the major portion of loan payments is applied to interest rather than principal during the early years of the loan. The other factor that will influence the timing of the sale is appreciation rate. Houses tend to appreciate in value quite rapidly when there is a supply/demand imbalance or when the area is developing with a significant influx of new people. After the situation stabilizes, however, and housing availability catches up with demand, a period of stability or even stagnation may ensue. This depends upon whether overbuilding occurs and the rate at which the area continues to grow. It is also possible to enter a period of economic decline. Cities in which employment levels fluctuate with the fortunes of a few large firms are particularly vulnerable. At any rate, once it becomes apparent that the local economy is entering a low-growth phase or a period during which housing appreciation rates will settle to low or modest levels, it may be time to sell. Remember, the primary source of gain generated by rental houses is usually the appreciation in value that takes place over time rather than the rental income that is generated. When a good rate of appreciation is no longer probable for the intermediate or long term, it is better to extract the equity and invest in something else.

Even if the growth outlook remains favorable, it may still be desirable to sell the house after five or six years in order to better leverage investment funds. For example, assume that you purchase a house for $100,000 at terms involving 20 percent down and the $80,000 balance to be repaid at 10 percent interest over a 25-year period. At this point, the investment is pretty well leveraged. A $20,000 down payment controls a $100,000 investment. Assume that the house appreciates in value at the rate of 15 percent per year for the next five years. By the end of five years, the value of the house will have increased to over $201,000. In addition, the loan balance will have been reduced to $75,280. Your equity at this point is the difference between the current market value and the balance owed on the purchase contract, or $125,720 ($201,000 minus $75,280). The degree of leverage has therefore changed substantially. Your equity position has increased from the original 20 percent to 62.5 percent of the house value ($125,720 is 62.5 percent of the current market value of $201,000).

Selling the house is one way to extract the equity. Refinancing is another option that may make sense provided the outlook for the area is for continued favorable rates of appreciation in housing. If the outlook for future appreciation rates in the area is not promising, it may be better to extract your funds and invest in something other than housing. Assuming that the housing growth outlook for the area is favorable and that the best investment strategy is to reinvest funds made available in other rental houses rather than in some other type of investment, then refinancing is a logical option to consider. In order to determine whether it is the best option, it is necessary to determine prevailing refinancing costs. Refinancing may involve prepayment penalties, loan and appraisal fees, and closing costs, since you are now both seller and buyer. Check with the bank or company that has the loan on the property and request an itemization of refinancing costs. Next, compare these costs with the costs of selling, including real estate fee, closing costs, and the loss of income that will be incurred if the house is vacated, cleaned up, and then left empty until a buyer is located. Refinancing may or may not be the best approach, depending upon the outcome of this comparison.

Another consideration concerning refinancing is that it permits deferral of the capital gains tax. If you are in a high tax bracket, it may be desirable to defer the sale until such time when either your gross or taxable income is relatively low. For this reason, refinancing may be a particularly good technique for investors who are not too many years away from retirement (again, provided appreciation rates in housing remain relatively high, making rental housing an attractive investment). Presumably, reduced income at retirement will result in a lower tax bracket and permit liquidation of properties at a time of minimal tax exposure.

Selling Tips

When you decide to sell, there are a few simple rules to keep in mind. First, it is probably wise to let a real estate agent handle the sale. Unless you are retired or available to spend the time to aggressively advertise and show the house to prospective buyers, the additional time required to sell, due to reduced buyer exposure, may substantially offset the cost of a real estate commission. Remember, if the house is empty during this period, mortgage payments continue, and there is no offsetting rental income being generated. Further, the individual who buys directly from the seller usually hopes to get a better deal since he or she knows there is no real estate commission involved. In other words, the do-it-yourself approach attracts bargain hunters.

The house should be in good, clean condition. The inside should be freshly painted, as well as the outside if it needs it. The floors should also be in good condition. Hardwood floors should be buffed, using a sanding machine with a steel wool pad and a good cleaning solution, and possibly refinished. If they are really bad, they may need professional refinishing. Carpets should be cleaned or, if necessary, replaced. There are usually opportunities to buy carpeting at substantial discounts through outlets that sell seconds or handle roll ends at greatly reduced prices. Other repairs that are relatively inexpensive but that significantly increase the appearance should also be made. Replace cheap lighting fixtures, broken wall switches, and broken windows, and get the lawn and landscaping in tip-top shape. It may also pay to refinish the kitchen cabinets if they need it. Most of these repairs can be done using relatively inexpensive help. If you live near a university or community college, there are always students looking for this type of work. All that is necessary is to contact the school office and ask them to place a card on their bulletin board advertising the employment opportunity. The objective is to get the house in shape as quickly as possible. For this reason, it may be desirable to hire five or six students at one time.

In some cases, it may be possible to place the house on the market while it is still occupied by the tenant, depending upon the attitude and willingness of the tenant. If the tenant is willing, limit the time that the house is available for showing to certain days and periods of the day compatible with the tenant's schedule and convenience. By extending this courtesy to the tenant, the chances of cooperation and of the house being in presentable condition are much improved. Some financial inducement may also be offered to the tenant, such as a reduction in monthly rent or, better yet, a bonus when the house is sold.

There are times when it pays to make major repairs before putting the house on the market. For example, if the roof needs replacement, the buyer will need to come up with the cash to pay for such work, in addition to the down payment and other costs involved in buying the house. If the seller replaces the roof prior to selling the house, and increases the selling price to cover this added cost, the buyer will have slightly higher mortgage payments but will not be required to come up with the cash outlay to replace the roof. This can be a major factor in selling the house. Many buyers will turn away from houses that require a large cash outlay for repairs, but will not have a problem with a higher sales price that fairly reflects such improvements. Moreover, buyers tend to overstate the cost of such repairs and attempt to negotiate price reductions that are larger than the actual cost of such work. So, on major cost items that inspectors or appraisers for lending institutions are likely to identify as required repairs in order to secure loan approval, it is better for the seller to correct such items before placing the house on the market.

Condominium Units

Individual condominium units that are leased or rented are similar to rental houses from an investment standpoint, and the preceding discussion is generally applicable. Individual condominium units investment refers to the purchase of one or more dwelling units within the condominium complex, rather than the entire complex itself. There are some differences, of course, but the profitability charts for rental houses may be used as a general guideline to determine profitability potential on a preliminary screening basis.

One of the advantages of condominium units over rental houses is that the rent-to-price ratio tends to be more favorable. This is because it costs less on a square-foot basis to build condominium units than single family houses. This is also true of duplexes, fourplexes, and multiple-family dwelling units in general.

There are also disadvantages with condominium units. The potential appreciation rate may well be less favorable than that of single family houses. Spiraling building costs have resulted in a shift to proportionately more condominiums in many parts of the country, as opposed to single family houses, particularly for dwellings in the low to medium price range. Apartment and condominium units cost less to build on a square-foot basis. They also cost less to heat and tend to be more conveniently located. For these and other reasons, it is possible that the era of single family housing will give way increasingly to condominium living. If so, it is reasonable to expect that modestly priced single family housing will appreciate at a high rate, particularly housing that is relatively close to major metropolitan areas. Such housing may well be at a premium in the future and become the dream of many condominium dwellers who want the privacy and independence of their own home and lot. From an investment standpoint, therefore, single family houses may be more profitable than individual condominium units, in spite of the less favorable rent-to-price ratio.

Another potential problem with condominium units is the reduction in investor control. Building and grounds maintenance for condominiums is typically accomplished under a maintenance contract administered by some representative body on behalf of the owners. Often, the developer or builder retains this lucrative contract. The cost for this service may be substantially higher than it should be, but it is usually difficult to get the consensus necessary among the owners to make a change. At best, it involves a lot of coordination and time.

A third concern about condominium rental units is that they are more susceptible to fluctuations in housing demand than single family houses. During boom periods when rental vacancies are low, condominium units may be great. Unfortunately, most booms are eventually followed by some type of bust or softening, typically brought about by a combination of regional economic reversals and/or overbuilding of housing units. When this happens, condominium units may be harder to keep occupied than single family houses.

Chart Section

Rental House
Profitability Analysis Charts

Worksheet—Rental Houses

This worksheet form may be used for each prospective investment to summarize the data required to use the charts that follow, as well as to compile input data needed for a more detailed profitability and cash flow analysis to be performed by the real estate firm or financial advisor of your choice. Permission is granted to make copies of the form.

Rental Houses

Property Identification: _____

Data for Using the Charts:

1. Price ($) _____

2. Monthly rent ($) _____

3. Estimated annual appreciation rate _____

4. Investor tax bracket (%) _____

5. Interest rate (6% or 9%, whichever is closer)_____

6. Estimated hold period (years) _____

7. Monthly rent as % of price = $\dfrac{\text{Item 2}}{\text{Item 1}}$ = _____ × 100 = _____%

Additional Data for Detailed Profitability and Cash Flow Analysis:

8. Installment contract or mortgage period (years) _____

9. Down payment ($ or %) _____

10 Annual operating expenses (taxes, maintenance, repairs, $) _____

11. Purchase fees ($ or % of price)_____

12. Selling expense at time of sale (% of selling price)_____

13. Interest rate on installment contract or mortgage (%) _____

14. Loan period (years) _____

WORKSHEET 5–1

Rental Houses

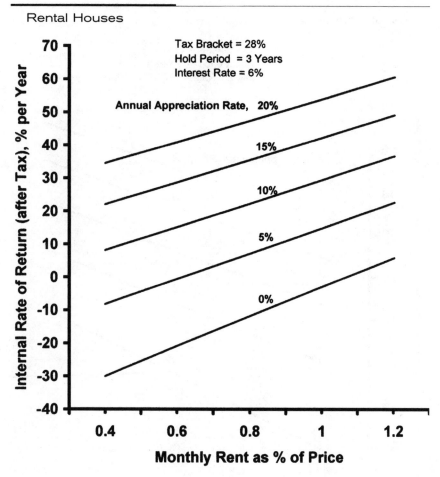

Monthly Rent as % of Price

WORKSHEET 5–2

Rental Houses

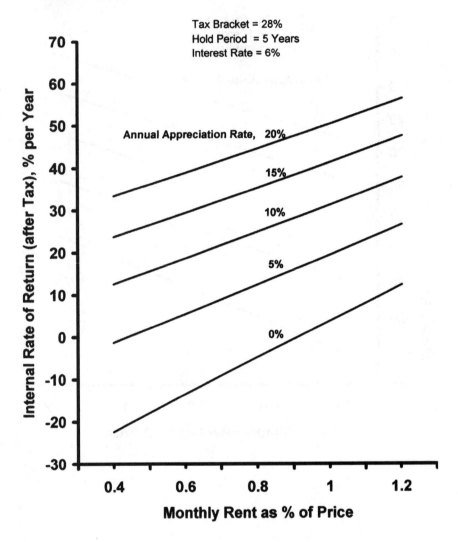

Tax Bracket = 28%
Hold Period = 5 Years
Interest Rate = 6%

WORKSHEET 5-3

Rental Houses

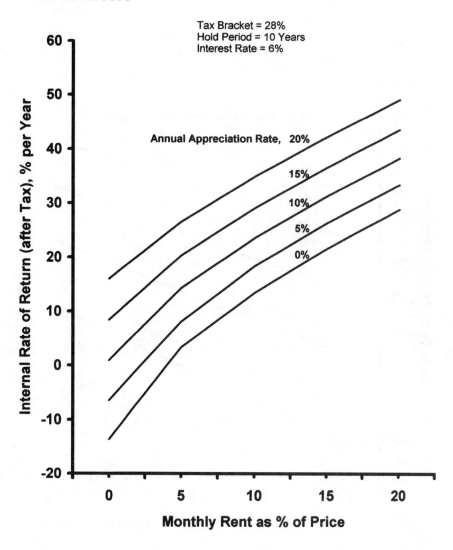

Tax Bracket = 28%
Hold Period = 10 Years
Interest Rate = 6%

Annual Appreciation Rate, 20%

15%

10%

5%

0%

Internal Rate of Return (after Tax), % per Year

Monthly Rent as % of Price

WORKSHEET 5-4

Rental Houses

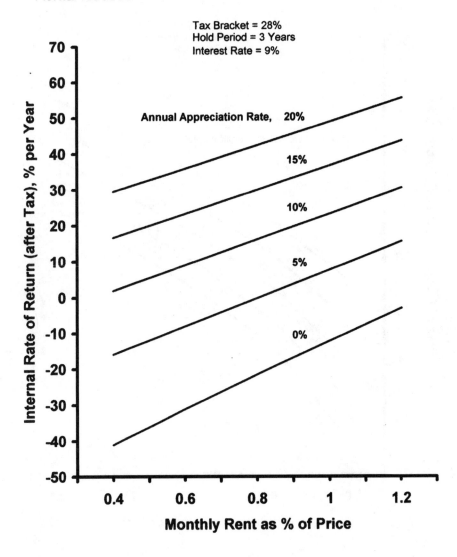

Tax Bracket = 28%
Hold Period = 3 Years
Interest Rate = 9%

WORKSHEET 5-5

Rental Houses

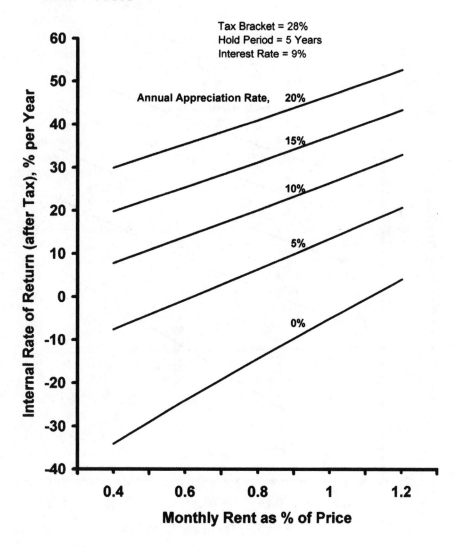

WORKSHEET 5-6

Rental Houses

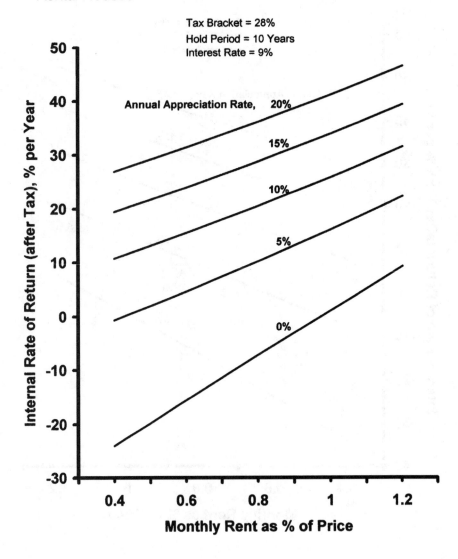

WORKSHEET 5–7

Rental Houses

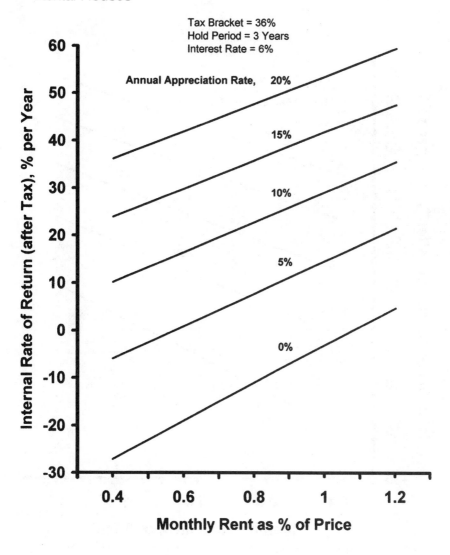

Tax Bracket = 36%
Hold Period = 3 Years
Interest Rate = 6%

Annual Appreciation Rate, 20%

15%

10%

5%

0%

Internal Rate of Return (after Tax), % per Year

Monthly Rent as % of Price

WORKSHEET 5-8

Rental Houses

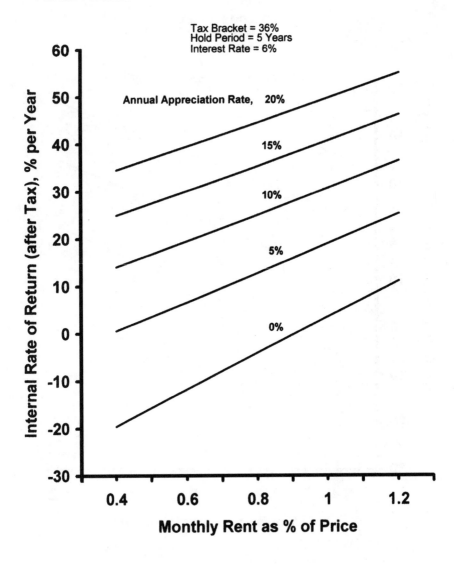

Tax Bracket = 36%
Hold Period = 5 Years
Interest Rate = 6%

WORKSHEET 5–9

Rental Houses

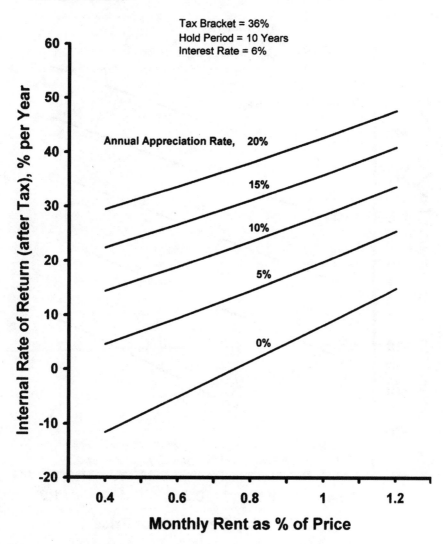

WORKSHEET 5—10

Rental Houses

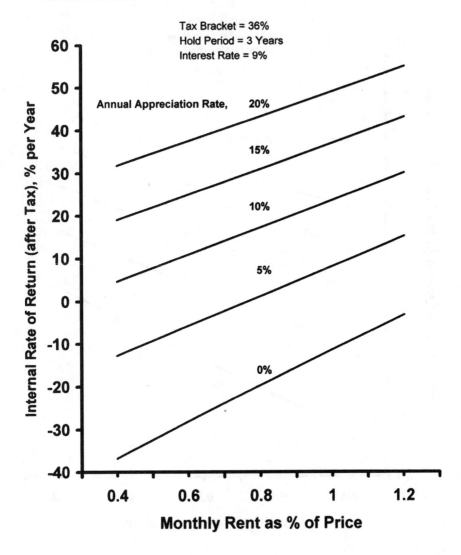

WORKSHEET 5–11

Rental Houses

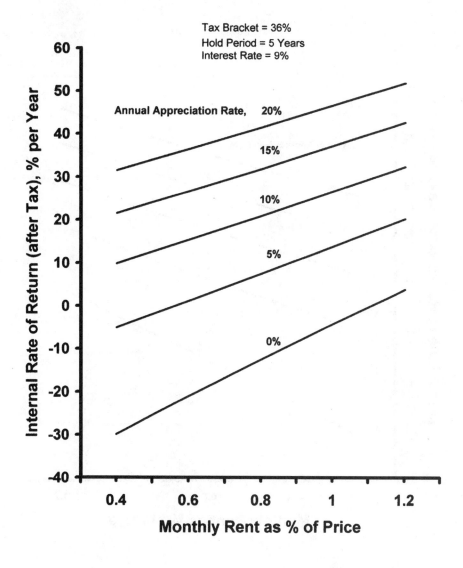

WORKSHEET 5–12

Rental Houses

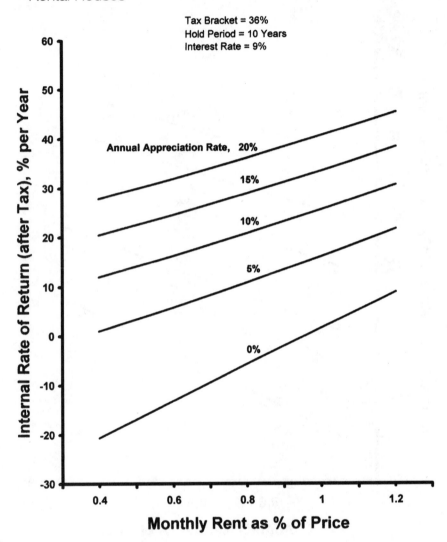

Tax Bracket = 36%
Hold Period = 10 Years
Interest Rate = 9%

Annual Appreciation Rate, 20%

15%

10%

5%

0%

Internal Rate of Return (after Tax), % per Year

Monthly Rent as % of Price

Assumptions Used for Rental House Charts

The following assumptions were used in compiling the preceding graphs:

1. Fees incurred at purchase (legal, escrow, loan fee): **2 percent of purchase price.**

2. Down payment at purchase: **20 percent of purchase price.**

3. Purchase price distribution for depreciation calculations: **building—80 percent; lot—20 percent.**

4. Loan period: **25 years.**

5. Depreciation: **27.5 years, straight line (building).**

6. Terms at resale: **cash.**

7. Operating costs (maintenance, repairs, taxes, insurance): **4 percent of property value, increasing annually at the same rate that the property appreciates in value.**

8. Monthly rent: **net after vacancies, and assumed to increase annually at the same rate that the property appreciates in value.**

9. Selling expenses incurred at resale (real estate commission, excise tax, recording fees, title insurance, points, etc.): **10 percent of selling price.**

10. Capital gains tax rate: **20 percent.** *Note:* It is recognized that capital gains tax rates are subject to change from those in effect at this writing. Refer to Appendix C for the effect of alternate capital gains tax rates on profitability.

CHAPTER 6

Lease/Option Strategy

Leasing property with an option to buy is a strategy for buying and selling houses with minimal or no cash outlay, both in terms of down payment and carrying costs. It involves leasing the property at a negotiated rental rate with the option to buy within a specified period of time at a prenegotiated price. It also requires the seller to assign the right to the investor to sublease and sell the property. After leasing the house, the investor subleases it to a sublessee with an option to buy within a specified period of time at a predefined price. The sale price specified for the house in the option agreement between the investor and the sublessee must obviously exceed the sale price specified in the option agreement between the investor and the owner. The monthly rent paid by the sublessee to the investor is also set at a level that is higher than, or at the very least comparable to, the rental rate paid by the investor to the owner. All of this requires that the investor locate properties that can be leased with an option to buy under very favorable terms. Since the rent received by the investor by sublease covers or exceeds the rental cost paid by the investor to the owner, it allows the investor to carry the property at no net cost or at a modest gain while waiting for the property to sell. It accomplishes this at minimal risk and, apart from ownership of the property, eliminates the need to obtain mortgage financing and avoids such costs as taxes, utilities, and major repairs or maintenance. Summing it up, this strategy seeks to produce gain for the investor in two ways: first, by the difference in the rent paid by the investor versus the rental income received; and secondly, by the difference in the prenegotiated sale price of the investor's buy option versus the buy option price provided by the investor to the sublessee.

An obvious question that arises is: Why would the owner of a house provide rental and purchase option terms that are more favorable than those the investor is able to obtain? Or, asked another way: Why would a renter or sublessee agree to terms that are less favorable than those the investor is able to obtain from the owner? Part of the answer has to do with the shorter time horizon of owners seeking to sell property, or to at least be relieved of the carrying costs pending such sale, or of renters seeking a place to live, compared to the longer time horizon of investors under this strategy. To illustrate, the owner of a house may be required to relocate a long distance away on short notice due to a job change. If the real estate market is slow, the owner faces the prospect of having the house on the market for an indeterminate and possibly prolonged period of time before it sells. This may put the owner in a financial bind. Faced with ongoing mortgage payments concurrent to costs incurred in establishing a new residence, the uncertainty and financial stress could require the consideration of other options, such as leasing the property. In this context, and particularly in a slow market, a relatively long-term lease (i.e., three to five years) with an option for the lessee to buy within that time frame for a set price could be very appealing. The owner avoids the uncertainty of delay in selling the house, the problem of renting the house from a long distance away, or the alternative of incurring the cost of a property management firm to handle the rental. The lease provides immediate cash flow relief to the owner through rental income, plus the prospect for sale at a fair price during the term of the lease. A lease/option agreement also typically provides some up-front cash in the form of a security deposit and financial consideration concerning the buy option. Another scenario that describes why an owner might find a lease/option appealing is when the house has been on the market for a long period of time but has failed to sell. Houses that remain unsold for long periods tend to become "stale," in real estate lingo, and cease to get very much action in terms of sales effort. A relatively long-term lease with an option to buy takes it off the market either until better times arrive or until the lessee exercises the option to buy. In the meantime, the owner receives a reasonable cash inflow through rental income. Still another reason for owner interest in the lease/option arrangement might be the desire to delay sale for tax reasons.

From a potential sublessee perspective, there can be several reasons for interest in a lease with an option to buy. Prospective sublessees are often newcomers to an area who would like to buy a house but are not in a financial position to do so until their current house is sold. Market conditions might be such that this could take a number of months. In order to avoid an interim move and the attendant storage and moving costs, the lease/option approach offers considerable appeal. Or, it may involve a young couple desirous of buying their first house but without having yet accumulated the necessary funds for the down payment. The lease/option arrangement in which the monies paid for the security deposit and to bind the agreement, together with a part of the rent, are applied as a credit to the purchase price or down payment, would contribute toward this need. In the meantime, the couple would be able to move into the house right away, avoid a double move, and the house would likely appreciate in value during the interim rental period prior to purchase.

The basic variables involved in lease/option transactions and their applicability to both the investor/owner and investor/sublessee transactions are as indicated below.

	Transaction Between:	
Variable	Investor & Owner	Investor & Sublessee
Option buy price	X	X
Lease period	X	X
Option cost and security deposit	X	X
Monthly rent	X	X
Rental credit upon buy		X
Fix-up costs	X	

The objective of the investor is to negotiate values for the owner/investor transaction variables listed above that are sufficiently more favorable than those negotiated for the investor/sublessee transaction to provide the outlook for a good financial gain. Achieving this provides the prospect for a positive cash flow during the hold period plus a significant gain when the house is sold. The first step by the investor in accomplishing this when a candidate property is located is to understand the market and the terms that are realistic under an investor/sublessee contract for the house in question. This involves determining the market value of the house based on comparable sales in the area, the going rental rate for such houses, the fix-up costs to make the house appealing and rentable, and any major repair needs that may exist. This will take some research and is best accomplished if the investor is familiar with real estate in the area involved. Once realistic values have been determined, the investor is in a position to determine the values necessary for variables describing the investor/owner transaction in order to make the projected scenario attractive from an investment perspective.

GUIDELINES TO THE LEASE/OPTION STRATEGY

James Lumley, in his book *5 Magic Paths to Making a Fortune in Real Estate* (John Wiley & Sons, Inc., 2000), treats the lease/option strategy in considerable depth, and his book is recommended reading for those interested in the lease/option approach. He advocates adhering to a number of key rules for this investment strategy. The essence of his suggested rules are reflected in the guidelines listed below, which make it clear that the lease/option strategy requires careful analysis and research to find the right opportunities. It also requires effective negotiations to put a deal in place that offers the prospect for a profitable outcome.

1. Buy wholesale, not retail. To begin with, this means that the purchase price must be discounted by the amount of the real estate commission (6 to 7 percent), the cost of which is built into the asking price but which the owner will not pay under the lease/option arrangement. In addition, another 10 percent or more off fair market value should be sought, at least on the initial offer. This assumes no major repair costs on the part of the investor.

2. Determine the fair market value through appropriate analysis. This implies comparative market analysis (CMA) for the local area (see Chapter 12 for more discussion).

3. Offer rental credits to the sublessee that can be applied against the purchase price. This is an effective marketing technique to encourage the sublessee to exercise the buy option. The up-front security deposit and fee paid for the buy option should also be offered as a credit against the purchase price as added incentive to buy.

4. The rent paid by the investor to the owner should be at a significant discount from the market level (Lumley advocates a 25 percent discount). This is not unreasonable since the lease is for a relatively long period of time, relieving the owner of the cost of refurbishing and periods of vacancy during tenant changes.

5. Limit any rental deposit to no more than one month's rent.

6. Avoid paying a fee to the owner for the option to buy, unless he or she insists on such payment. The target limitation on such a fee is no more than one month's rent and should be credited toward the purchase price. Try to get the owner to accept such fee payment, if required, in the form of prepaid rent.

7. The contract between the investor and the owner should provide for the investor's right to sublease apart from the owner's permission.

8. Preferably, structure the investor/owner contract to be consummated after the investor has found a sublessee tenant.

9. Generally avoid investor/owner deals that do not extend over one year. Four to six years is recommended.

10. Seek the right to renew the buy option from the owner for a modest monetary consideration.

11. Avoid deals on properties requiring major repairs unless paid for by the owner.

12. Limit lease/option strategy to single family houses.

13. Include a clause in the owner/investor contract that gives the investor the right to assign the investor's position.

14. Verify that there are no liens or judgments against the property and that the owner is contractually committed to make mortgage payments. Include a provision that permits the investor to make such payments directly to the mortgage holder and be credited from lease payments to the owner.

15. Have a good attorney draw up separate agreements between the investor and the owner and the investor and the sublessee.

How It Would Work

Using a hypothetical example to illustrate the lease/option strategy, assume that the investor locates a house for which the owner is willing to establish a lease/option agreement. After researching the property, the investor determines that the owner's asking price of $150,000 represents a realistic current market value. The investor further determines that comparable houses in the area are renting for about $1000 a month. A front-end deposit of $3000 is typical to cover the security deposit and the option to buy such a house within two years. This payment would typically be credited against the buy price at the time of purchase, along with a $200 per month rental credit.

With this information in mind, the investor is now in a position to establish negotiating goals concerning the transaction with the owner. Referring to the guidelines, the investor might offer a five-year lease/option arrangement involving a buy option price of $126,900. This reduction of $23,100 from the $150,000 asking price takes into account the fact that the asking price has built into it a 6 percent real estate commission of $9000 that the seller will not have to pay. The offer also incorporates a 10 percent reduction, or $14,100, of the $141,000 balance after deducting the real estate commission. From the owner's perspective this $14,100 is the real reduction in income from the sale relative to the asking price. Assume that after negotiating the terms, the parties settle on a compromise buy option price of $130,000. The investor and the owner settle on a $3000 front-end payment to cover the security deposit and the option-to-buy provision, the total to be credited against the purchase price when the buy option is exercised. The investor offers to pay $500 in cosmetic fix-up costs and a monthly rent of $900.

This scenario is summarized below in terms of the transaction variables from the investor's perspective, both for the investor/owner and investor/sublessee transactions. The scenario assumes that the sublessee exercises the option to buy at the end of two years. The figures in parenthesis designate cash outflow. Figures not in parentheses designate cash inflow, all from the investor's perspective.

	Transaction Between:	
	Investor & Owner	**Investor & Sublessee**
Lease period	5 years	2 years
Option buy price	($130,000)	$150,000
Rental cost or income	($900 × 24 mos. =$21,600)	$1000 × 24 mos. =$24,000
Rental credit at buy		($200×24 mos.=$4800)
Security deposit	($3000)	3000
Security deposit credit at buy	$3000	($3000)
Fix-up costs	($500)	
Totals	($152,100)	$169,200
Two-year gain:	$169,200−$152,100=$17,100	

Under the scenario, if all went as planned, the investor would end up with a net gain of $17,100 over two years with virtually no investment or holding costs. There are risks involved, of course, but they are not substantial provided a favorable deal is negotiated. For example, assume that the real estate market softens and the sublessee does not exercise the option to buy and moves out at the end of the two-year lease. The investor would still have netted $2400 ($24,000−$21,600) in rental income at no investment other than the original $500 fix-up costs during the two-year period. Additional costs would be incurred after the sublessee vacates the house, however, for refurbishment and in the form of lost rental income during the period it is vacant. The investor would then need to find another sublessee with an option to buy. Very likely, the real estate market would firm up over the next few years, making a desirable sale possible and putting the strategy back on track. So, while the risk of financial loss is minimal, it remains a possibility due to the unpredictable and can involve a significant amount of time and effort that we have not priced into the scenario. On the positive side, the concept utilizes leverage to a very high degree, and investors who master the strategy enjoy the possibility of putting together a number of such deals at very low cost, which collectively offer the prospect of producing a very good income.

CHAPTER 7

Apartment Houses

Apartment houses are similar in many respects to rental houses from an investment perspective, but there are also important differences. One is the relatively favorable rent-to-price ratio of apartments versus rental houses. This results from the fact that apartment houses cost less to build than rental houses on a square-foot basis. Other differences include maintenance costs, location considerations, resale market, and renter types.

CASH FLOW PROFILE

Because of construction and operating-cost economies, the typical cash flow profile for apartment building investments is somewhat different from that of rental houses. In general, they provide a much more favorable net annual cash flow pattern and significant income during the hold period. To illustrate, consider the cash flow pattern for an apartment house investment described by the following assumptions:

Price:	400,000
Gross income:	$50,000 per year
Expenses:	$15,000 per year

Purchase terms:
Down payment:	20 percent
Interest rate:	6 percent
Mortgage period:	25 years
Depreciation method:	Straight line
Investor tax bracket:	28 percent
Annual appreciation rate:	5 percent
Hold period prior to resale:	10 years

Figure 7-1 illustrates the annual after-tax cash flow for this example.

Note that immediately following the large initial investment of $88,000 (down payment and purchase fees), a positive net annual cash flow is achieved. This net cash inflow increases each year, reaching about $20,000 by the ninth year. This increase occurs because inflation permits the rents to be adjusted upward each year, while mortgage payments remain constant. Operating costs also increase annually with inflation, but not enough to offset the improving cash flow trend resulting from these other factors. The large inflow during the tenth year reflects the net after-tax gain as the equity is liquidated through resale. The equity is built up over the 10-year period through mortgage payments that reduce the loan balance and through the appreciation in value of the property. Figure 7-2 illustrates the cash flow for the same example on a cumulative basis.

Note that the cumulative cash outlay gradually diminishes due to successive net annual inflows and that break-even is achieved by the seventh year. The apartment is sold at the end of the tenth year and the accumulated equity is liquidated, resulting in a large cash inflow. This cash flow pattern typifies a successful apartment house investment and demonstrates the appeal to investors who are looking for a modest annual income and want to avoid a cash drain during the hold period. Note that in terms of a long-term negative cash flow position, the apartment house investment is more favorable than that of the rental house example of Chapter 5 (Figures 5-4 and 5-5), even though the annual appreciation rate assumed for the apartment house was only 5 percent, compared to 10 percent in the rental house illustration. As with rental houses, however, much of the gain occurs in the form of equity buildup and is deferred until the property is sold. The after-tax average annual rate of return produced by the investment in this illustration is approximately 23 percent.

FIGURE 7-1

Net Annual Cash Flow After Tax, Typical Apartment
Investment

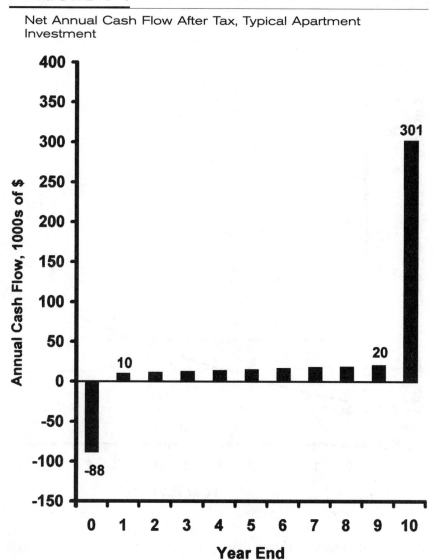

BASIC INFORMATION REQUIREMENTS FOR ESTIMATING PROFITABILITY

Estimating the expected return on investment for apartment houses involves a slightly different approach from that used for rental houses. The primary variables involved in using the rental house

FIGURE 7–2

Cumulative Net Cash Flow After Tax, Typical Apartment
Investment

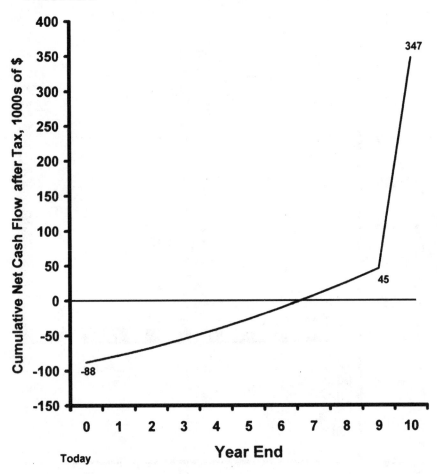

profitability analysis charts were price, rental income, and appreciation rate. Operating costs, such as maintenance, repairs, and taxes,
were assumed to vary as a function of price, and representative values were factored into the calculations used to produce the charts.
In the case of apartment houses, there is considerable variation in
operating costs depending upon building size, age, condition, type
of construction, location, and many other factors. Accordingly, the

relationship of operating costs to price is not sufficiently uniform to warrant a similar approach. Instead, it is necessary to scope operating costs, in addition to price, rental income, and appreciation rate, in order to predict profitability. Of course, there are other variables that also influence the expected rate of return, such as down payment, investor tax bracket, mortgage interest rate, and the number of years the apartment house is held prior to sale. However, these secondary variables usually do not require a great deal of judgment or research. In most cases they are accommodated by the profitability analysis charts as additional identifiable variables. Otherwise, representative assumptions have been factored into the calculations used to produce the charts.

Consider the following brief explanations of the more critical variables and items of information that must be determined in order to estimate potential profitability through the use of the profit analysis charts at the end of this chapter:

Gross Income

Gross income is defined as expected rather than potential total income derived from rents and other possible sources. Expected income will be less than potential income due to vacancies. In estimating gross income, therefore, it is necessary to take the anticipated vacancy rate into account. This is determined by recent rental experience for the apartment building in question, vacancy rates prevailing for local area apartments in general, and the future supply and demand outlook for rental units in the locality. In addition to rental income, apartment houses sometimes produce other income through coin-operated laundry equipment or other services for which fees are charged. Such nonrental income should also be included in the expected gross income.

Operating Expenses

These are the expenses incurred other than mortgage payments. Operating expenses typically cover such items as taxes, insurance, utilities (which are paid by the owner—not those paid directly by tenants), maintenance, repairs, equipment replacement, legal fees, accounting, management, etc. The only accurate way to determine these expenses is to examine the financial records maintained by the current owner. Records of this type must be maintained for tax purposes, and you should insist that they be made available for examination prior to a firm offer. In the event that the building is new and there is no prior history, or if the records are poorly maintained, some general guidelines are provided later in this chapter to help scope probable operating cost levels.

Appreciation Rate

As with rental houses, appreciation rate is simply the average annual percent increase in value anticipated for the apartment house during the period that it will be owned. In estimating the annual appreciation rate, keep in mind that apartment house investments tend to be held for longer periods of time than rental houses. This is because the market for apartment houses is more limited—they are sold to other investors, whereas rental houses are usually sold to home owners. In addition, apartment houses usually produce a net annual income that improves with time, as discussed earlier, and they tend to be purchased by the type of investor who has longer-term income objectives in mind. Rental houses, on the other hand, are often purchased to capitalize upon periods of good growth in values and tend to be turned over more frequently in order to periodically extract equity for reinvestment.

The profitability analysis charts for apartment houses reflect this consideration and assume a 10-year hold period from purchase to sale. The longer-term hold period that may be anticipated for apartment houses tends to make more conservative appreciation rate assumptions appropriate. Property values tend to grow in spurts or cycles in response to supply/demand imbalances. After the supply of housing units catches up to or exceeds demand in a specific locality, values tend to stabilize for a period of time until new economic developments or stimuli cause another growth spurt. The appreciation rate is intended to reflect a realistic annual average that spans the entire hold period. In the case of apartment buildings, this is likely to be of sufficient length to include periods of high growth as well as periods of relative stability or even economic decline.

In estimating appreciation rate, it is important to recognize that growth in market value will probably be lower than the rate of price increase for new apartment buildings. This is because buildings depreciate or wear out with the passage of time. The typical life expectancy for an apartment building is 40 years, and in the absence of inflation, it might be expected to decline in value by about one-fourth or 25 percent over a 10-year period, or about 2.5 percent each year. The land upon which it rests, however, will probably not decline in value. In estimating the probable annual appreciation rate of an apartment house investment, it is important to take into consideration the rate of inflation, the rate at which the land will increase in value, the rate at which new apartment house construction costs will escalate, and then offset these rates by the annual depreciation or decline in real value that occurs to the building as it becomes older.

USING THE PROFITABILITY ANALYSIS CHARTS

The profitability analysis charts at the end of the chapter make it possible to scope the probable rate of return on investment for apartment houses. As explained earlier, it is first necessary to determine or estimate values for price, appreciation rate, gross income, and operating costs. The investor tax bracket and interest rate are also needed. In using the charts, some of this information is translated into two basic ratios, as illustrated in Figure 7-3.

The bottom scale of the profit analysis chart is "Price as a Multiple of Gross Income." This is a ratio determined by dividing the price of the apartment house by the expected gross annual income. For example, if the price is $400,000 and the gross annual income is $50,000, the price expressed as a multiple of gross income is:

$$\frac{\$400,000 \quad \text{(Price)}}{\$50,000 \quad \text{(Gross Annual Income)}} = 8.0$$

The gross income is that which prevails at the time of purchase and does not reflect the future escalation anticipated over time due to inflation. This consideration has been taken into account in computing the charts, but need not concern you in using the charts.

Note that several curves are plotted on the chart for various ratios of expense to gross income. In order to determine which

FIGURE 7-3

Apartment Houses

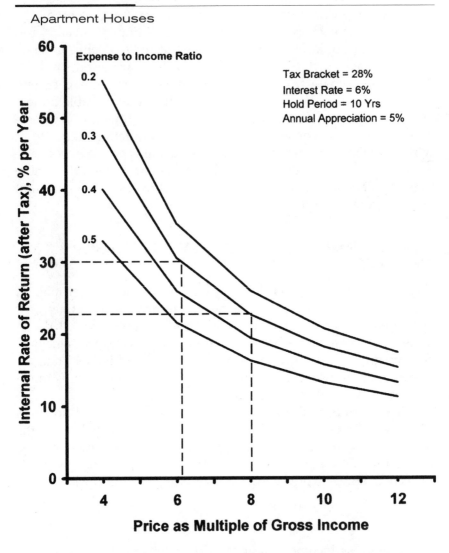

curve to use, simply divide the estimated annual operating expense by the expected gross annual income. For example, assuming that a study of available records indicates that expenses average $15,000 per year, this ratio would be computed as follows:

$$\frac{\$15,000 \ \text{(Annual Operating Expenses)}}{\$50,000 \ \text{(Gross Annual Income)}} = .3$$

The other variables, appreciation rate, investor's income tax bracket and interest rate, are accommodated by selecting the particular chart for the correct combination of these variables. In evaluating the investment, therefore, the first step involves selection of the chart that most closely accommodates these variables.

After selecting the proper chart, simply locate the price-to-income ratio on the bottom scale (8.0 in this example); locate where this value intersects the curve that most closely approximates the expense-to-income ratio (.3 in the example); and read off the return on investment on the left-hand vertical scale, as indicated in Figure 7-3. It is about 22 percent in this illustration.

If the after-tax rate of return on investment thus determined is below an acceptable level, the price is too high. In order to determine the price necessary to achieve an acceptable profitability, simply determine the value for the Price as Multiple of Gross Income (bottom scale of Figure 7-3) that corresponds to an acceptable after-tax return on investment (left scale) and multiply this value by the gross income. For example, if you want to achieve a 30 percent return on investment in the Figure 7-3 example, the price as a multiple of gross income must equal 6. A horizontal line drawn from the 30 percent point on the left-hand vertical scale intersects the proper Expense to Income Ratio curve (.3 in this example) at a point corresponding to a value of 6 on the bottom scale. Since the gross income is $50,000, the price that is compatible with this factor is 6 × $50,000 = $300,000.

TYPICAL OPERATING EXPENSE RATIOS

As suggested earlier, determining the operating expense level requires examining the financial records for the past several years. What follows are some general guidelines concerning typical values for operating expenses as a percent of gross income for several different types of apartment house situations. However, these typical values should not be used in your analysis. Actual values must be determined if the evaluation is to be meaningful.

Category	Typical Description	Ratio of Expenses to Income
A	New/developing neighborhood Prime modern building	.35

Category	Typical Description	Ratio of Expenses to Income
B	Prime rent levels High-caliber tenants Equilibrium neighborhood Passed peak of development More recent and more desirable developments exist	.50
C	Moderate-income tenants Declining neighborhood Older building Low-income tenants	.67

THE 15 PERCENT RULE

There are other quick scoping techniques sometimes used by investors with regard to apartments to determine either financial acceptability or the maximum price that should be paid. We do not recommend any of them, but describe them briefly to alert you of their use and inadequacies. One of these is commonly referred to as the 15 percent rule, which states that the before-tax annual cash flow must equal at least 15 percent of the gross income. The before-tax cash flow is the gross potential annual income minus annual operating expenses and loan payment amounts.

Another way of stating the rule: The annual operating expenses plus loan payments should not exceed 85 percent of the annual gross potential income. To illustrate, consider an apartment house that has an annual gross potential income of $100,000, annual operating expenses of $40,000, and is priced at $500,000. The question is whether it is a good investment. Using the 15 percent rule, the initial step is to determine the cash flow by deducting the annual operating expenses and loan payments from the gross potential annual income. To do this, it is necessary to determine the annual loan payment amount, which can be done with the aid of a table of monthly mortgage loans (included in the Appendix). Based upon an asking price of $500,000, it would probably be necessary to pay 20 percent down, leaving a balance of $400,000. If prevailing loan terms provide a 25-year mortgage at 10 percent interest, the monthly mortgage payment would be $3634.88, or about $43,618 annually. The cash flow can now be computed using the 15 percent rule formula described earlier.

The annual cash flow would be the $100,000 gross potential income, less annual operating expenses of $40,000, less $43,618 per year in mortgage payments. A bit of arithmetic yields the answer of $16,382. This cash flow of $16,382 represents about 16 percent of the $100,000 gross annual income. Since this exceeds 15 percent, the price appears to be favorable using the 15 percent rule. This is intended only as a very preliminary scoping to determine whether more serious consideration and analysis are warranted. Unlike the profitability analysis charts, it fails to take into account such considerations as tax bracket, appreciation rate, and interest rate, and it does not provide the expected rate of return on investment. Although useful as a "hip pocket" preliminary scoping tool, it should not be used for making investment decisions.

CAPITALIZATION RATE

Another quick scoping technique sometimes used involves the capitalization rate ("cap rate") to estimate the value of income-producing property. The cap rate is defined as the net operating income as a percentage of the price or cost of the property. The net operating income, in turn, is the annual gross operating income less the annual operating expense. The annual operating expense does not include mortgage payments to finance the investment or the income taxes that must be paid. It does include such items as property taxes, insurance, utilities, maintenance, management, supplies, and similar expenses. Net operating income, therefore, is simply the average annual income generated each year, primarily from rent, less the annual cost to operate the apartment. If the apartment building is owned free and clear, and prior to the payment of income taxes, the net operating income would be the net income stream or financial gain that would be produced each year by the apartment. Expressing the cap rate as a formula, it looks like this:

$$\text{Capitalization Rate} = \frac{\text{Net Operating Income}}{\text{Price of Building}}$$

Rearranging the formula to compute the value of the property, it takes the following form:

$$\text{Price of Building} = \frac{\text{Net Operating Income}}{\text{Capitalization Rate}}$$

To illustrate its use, assume an apartment building is priced at $500,000 and produces a net annual operating income of $50,000 (rental income less operating expenses). The capitalization rate would be computed as follows:

$$\frac{\$50,000}{\$500,000} = .10 = 10\%$$

In other words, the apartment building produces an annual rate of return of 10 percent. Of course, this simplistic approach ignores depreciation, the resale value of the property at some future date, the time value of money, the cost of capital expenditures to improve the property, and the tax implications of the scenario. Accordingly, it is not a substitute for the internal rate of return calculations reflected in the worksheet charts at the end of the chapter. However, it is a quick scoping approach that is useful in comparing several investment options prior to conducting a more thorough analysis. It is also a statistic that real estate agents are likely to use as they present different possibilities for your consideration. For this reason alone it is important to understand the concept.

Capitalization rates tend to vary based on the overall desirability of the property in question. Higher cap rates would normally be expected for less-desirable properties since they represent higher risk. For example, investors may expect a cap rate of 12 percent as typical for average quality apartment buildings in a given area, but only 10 percent for top quality new buildings in prime locations.

To illustrate its use in computing the value of a given property, assume that the net annual operating income is $25,000 and the average cap rate in the neighborhood involved for buildings of comparable age and condition is about 12 percent. The value of the property is computed as follows:

$$\text{Price of Building} = \frac{\$25,000}{.12} \quad \begin{array}{l}\text{(Net Operating Income)}\\ \text{(Capitalization Rate)}\end{array}$$

$$= \$208,333$$

If the property is listed at a level close to this value, more thorough analysis and investigation would be justified.

GROSS RENT MULTIPLIER

Another "quickie" method sometimes used to establish the value of income property is called the gross rent multiplier (GRM). It is one of the least-desirable quick evaluation techniques and should be avoided. It is mentioned here only to alert you as to its inadequacies in the event that your real estate agent uses it as the basis for scoping the value of properties you may be considering. The GRM is simply the price of the property divided by the annual rental income. For example, an apartment building that recently sold for $400,000 and produced rental income of $65,000 annually would have a GRM of 6.2 ($400,000 divided by $65,000). Assume that a bit of research concerning recent sales of income properties comparable to what you are seeking revealed that the average GRM of such properties was about 6. The erroneous conclusion that might be reached is that similar properties on the market that have a GRM higher than 6 would likely represent good buys. Unfortunately, decisions based on such a conclusion could prove to be disastrous. The reason for this is that the operating expenses of such properties can vary widely, even though they may have comparable GRMs. The GRM approach totally ignores the operating expenses and can therefore be very misleading in terms of establishing value.

SIZE CONSIDERATIONS

The options concerning multifamily income properties range from duplexes to large complexes with many units. There are advantages and disadvantages to investing in each.

Duplexes are often appealing to first-time investors because of the relatively low price and low down payment required, particularly if the investor resides in one of the units. They are also small enough for the owner to manage, as well as take care of minor repairs. Duplexes reduce the cost of living for the investor who lives in one of the units by virtue of the income produced by the other unit. A potential disadvantage to owning and living in a duplex is the close proximity to your tenant, which can sometimes put a strain on the tenant/landlord relationship. Another obvious disadvantage is the limited income they produce because of their size. On the positive side, duplexes are usually easy to sell, as well as easy to rent. Tenants tend to prefer duplexes to large apartment complexes.

The next step up in apartment investments involves three- or four-unit apartment buildings—triplexes or quads. Like duplexes, if you plan to occupy one of the units, it is usually easier to find financing with a low down payment. They have the advantage of producing more income than duplexes, along with the prospects of producing a positive cash flow. Again, the reduced investment involved compared to larger complexes equates to lower risk and makes triplexes and quads good investments for inexperienced income property investors. These complexes are still small enough for the owner to manage, provided the time and inclination to do so exists. They also represent excellent stepping-stones to larger income properties as experience is acquired. Moreover, the owner-ship of several smaller apartment buildings instead of a single larg-er complex provides location diversification and spreads out the risk in terms of events that may detrimentally affect an area and make it less attractive to tenants. The impact on cash flow from a vacancy in triplexes and quads is dampened compared to duplex-es since the occupied units continue to produce income. Like duplexes, triplexes and quads are generally easier to sell and are more appealing to renters than large complexes, making it easier to keep them occupied and minimize turnover.

Moving up the ladder to apartments with more units shifts the investor into commercial-grade, as opposed to residential-grade, buildings. They offer a much higher earning potential and the opportunity for the investor to move into income property as a vocation, rather than an avocation. Larger complexes offer the prospects of carrying one or more vacancies (depending upon the number of units) and to still maintain a positive cash flow. Unlike smaller apartment complexes where the investor's income from his job may be a factor in obtaining financing, larger complexes generally stand on their own as commercial ventures from the perspective of the lending institution. Larger complexes typically require professional management. Management fees run at about 10 percent of the gross rental income, plus charges for special services such as yard maintenance, painting, repairs, etc. The larger the complex in terms of rental units, the more essential it is to hire a professional management firm. The owner who intends to manage the apartment apart from a management firm needs both good organizational and people skills. The management issues are extensive and time consuming. They include dealing with tenants, collecting rents, negotiating with contractors for needed repairs and maintenance work, maintaining records, filing, bookkeeping, and much more.

OTHER CONSIDERATIONS IN APARTMENT HOUSE INVESTING

There are many other important aspects of apartment house investment that are beyond the scope of this book, the focus of which is assessing potential profitability. Further study is advised, therefore, on the nonfinancial aspects of investing in apartments. Particularly critical is the issue of location. For rental houses, location considerations focus upon factors important to future home buyers, since the appreciation in value that occurs is of greater significance than rental income. Accordingly, tenant interests concerning location are subordinate to those of future home buyers.

In the case of apartment houses, however, value is largely a function of rental income in context with operating costs. In order to maintain high occupancy levels and high rental rates, which ensure both good income and resale potential, location considerations for apartment houses focus upon tenants' interests. This means good neighborhoods, convenient locations to shopping centers, and access to public transportation and major arterials. Preferably, apartments should be within walking distance to shopping areas for groceries, pharmaceuticals, and other day-to-day essentials.

Chart Section

Apartment Houses
Profitability Analysis Charts

Worksheet–Apartment Houses

This worksheet form may be used for each prospective investment to summarize the data required to use the charts that follow, as well as to compile input data needed for a more detailed profitability analysis and cash flow analysis to be performed by the real estate firm or financial advisor of your choice. Permission is granted to make copies of this form.

Worksheet Information—Apartment Houses

Property Identification: _____

Data for Using the Charts: _____

1. Price ($) _____

2. Gross annual income ($) _____

3. Annual operating expenses ($) _____

4. Estimated annual appreciation rate (%) _____

5. Investor tax bracket (%) _____

6. Interest rate (6% or 9%, whichever is closer)_____

7. Price as multiple of gross income $= \dfrac{\text{Item 1}}{\text{Item 2}} =$ _____

8. Expense-to-income ratio $= \dfrac{\text{Item 3}}{\text{Item 2}} =$ _____

Additional Data for Detailed Profitability and Cash Flow Analysis:

9. Installment contract or mortgage period (years) _____

10. Down payment ($ or %) _____

11. Purchase fees ($ or % of price)_____

12. Selling expense at time of sale (% of selling price)_____

13. Interest on installment contract or mortgage (%)_____

14. Loan period (years) _____

WORKSHEET 7–1

Apartment Houses

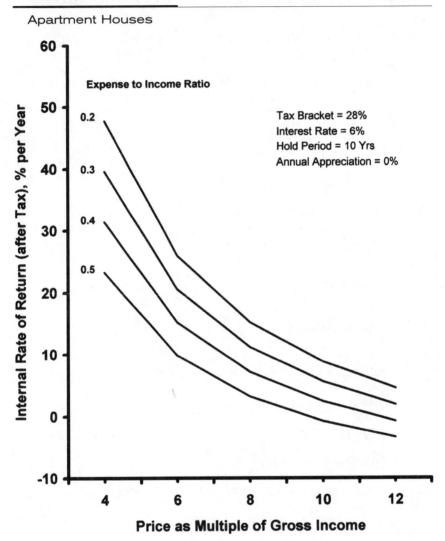

WORKSHEET 7-2

Apartment Houses

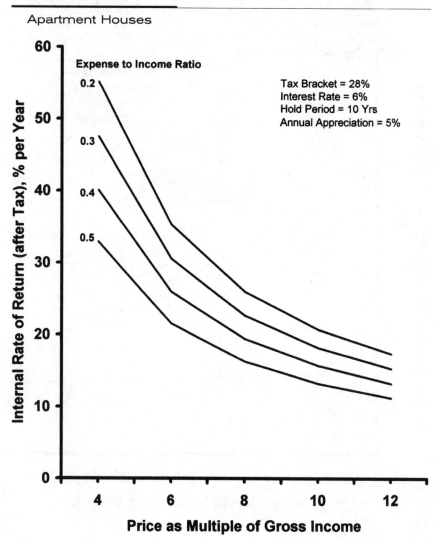

WORKSHEET 7-3

Apartment Houses

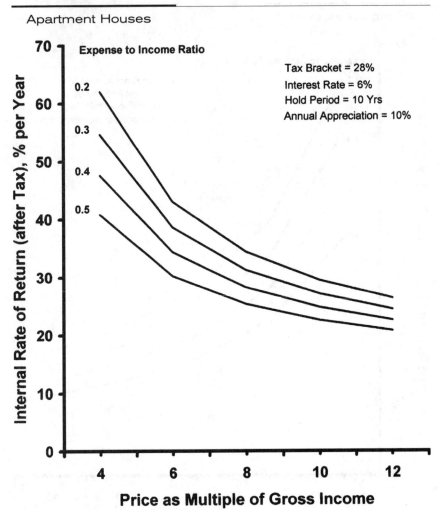

WORKSHEET 7–4

Apartment Houses

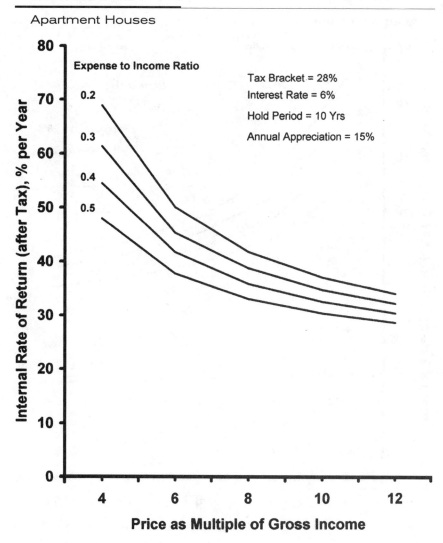

Expense to Income Ratio

Tax Bracket = 28%
Interest Rate = 6%
Hold Period = 10 Yrs
Annual Appreciation = 15%

WORKSHEET 7-5

Apartment Houses

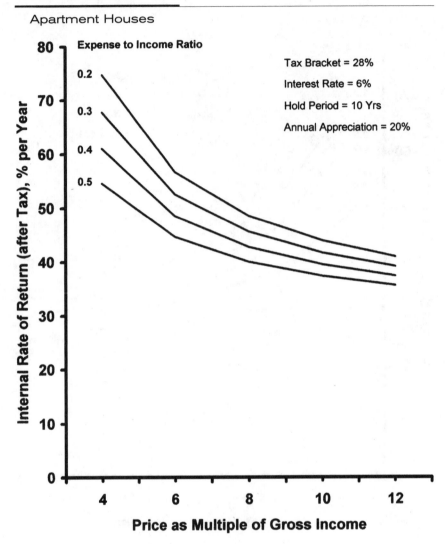

WORKSHEET 7-6

Apartment Houses

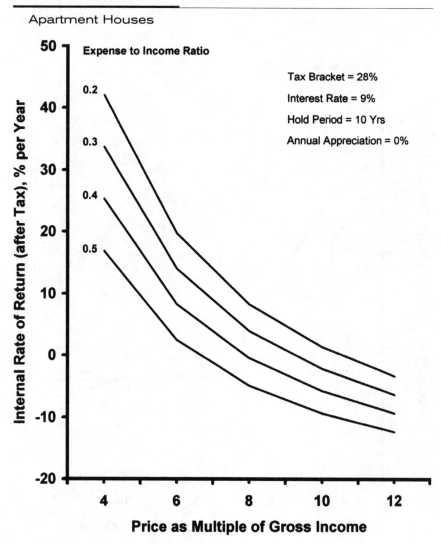

WORKSHEET 7-7

Apartment Houses

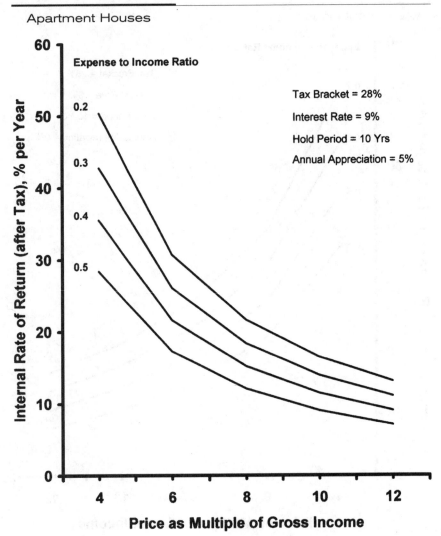

Price as Multiple of Gross Income

WORKSHEET 7–8

Apartment Houses

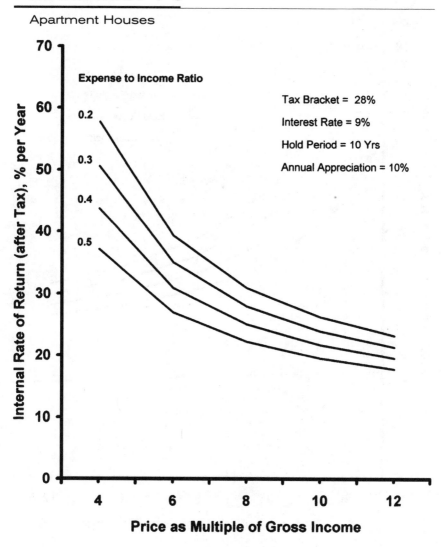

W O R K S H E E T 7–9

Apartment Houses

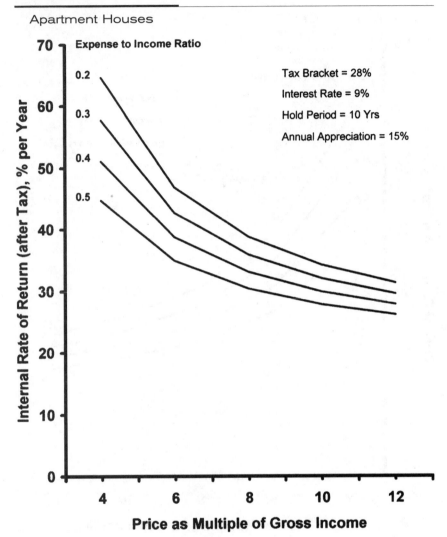

Tax Bracket = 28%
Interest Rate = 9%
Hold Period = 10 Yrs
Annual Appreciation = 15%

WORKSHEET 7-10

Apartment Houses

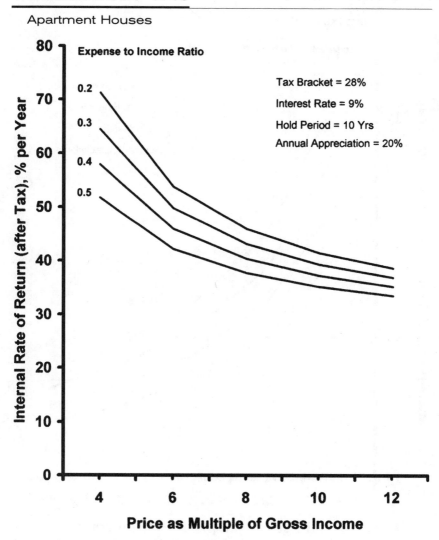

WORKSHEET 7–11

Apartment Houses

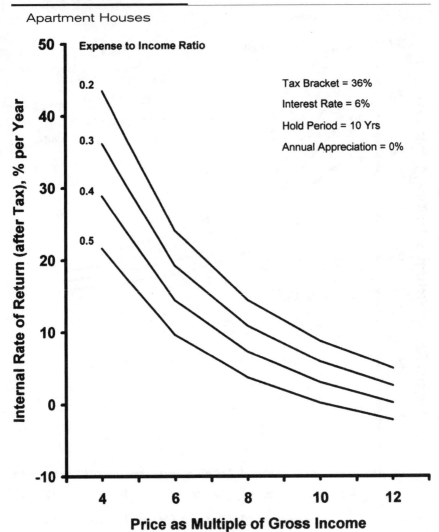

WORKSHEET 7–12

Apartment Houses

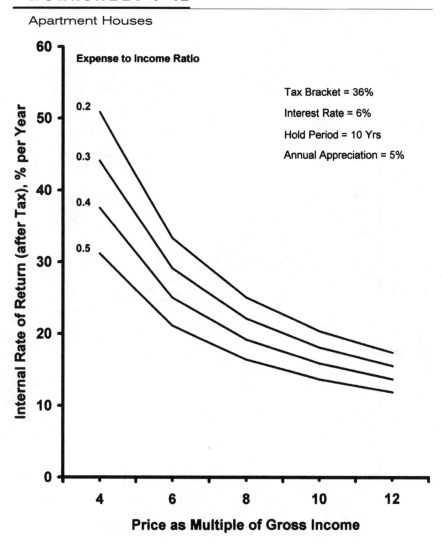

WORKSHEET 7-13

Apartment Houses

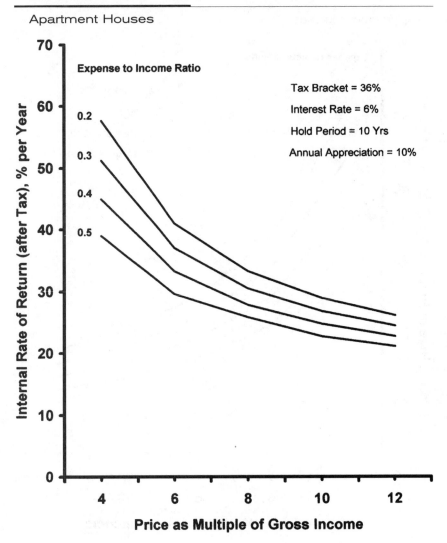

WORKSHEET 7–14

Apartment Houses

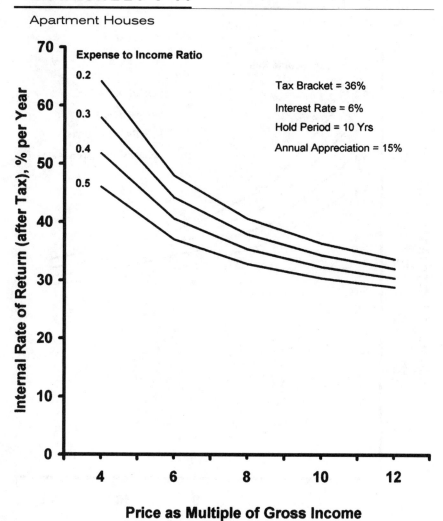

Price as Multiple of Gross Income

WORKSHEET 7–15

Apartment Houses

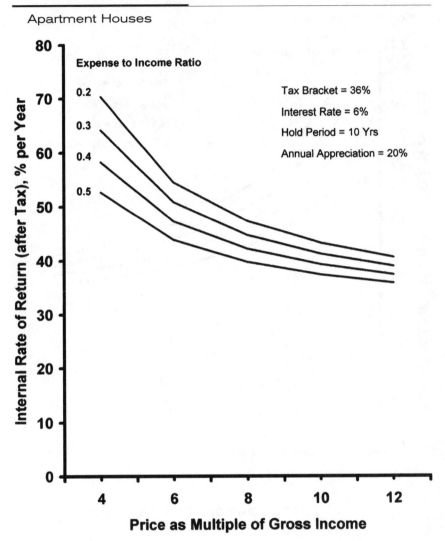

WORKSHEET 7–16

Apartment Houses

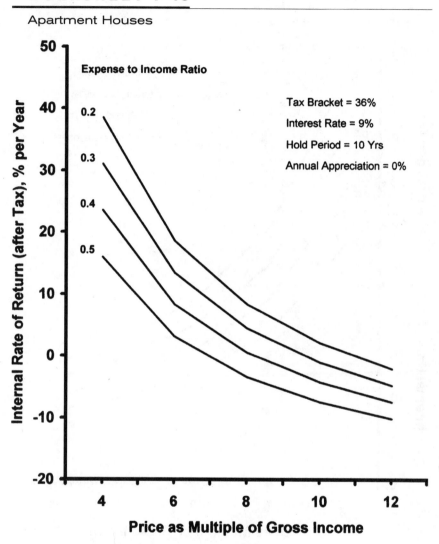

Internal Rate of Return (after Tax), % per Year

Expense to Income Ratio

Tax Bracket = 36%
Interest Rate = 9%
Hold Period = 10 Yrs
Annual Appreciation = 0%

Price as Multiple of Gross Income

WORKSHEET 7–17

Apartment Houses

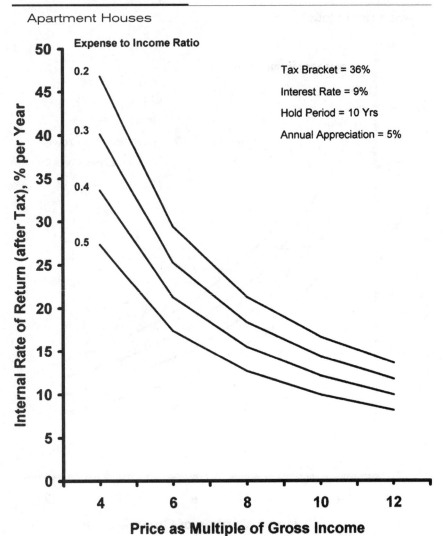

WORKSHEET 7–18

Apartment Houses

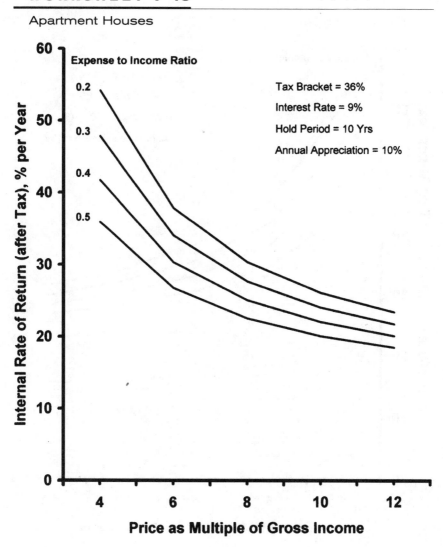

WORKSHEET 7–19

Apartment Houses

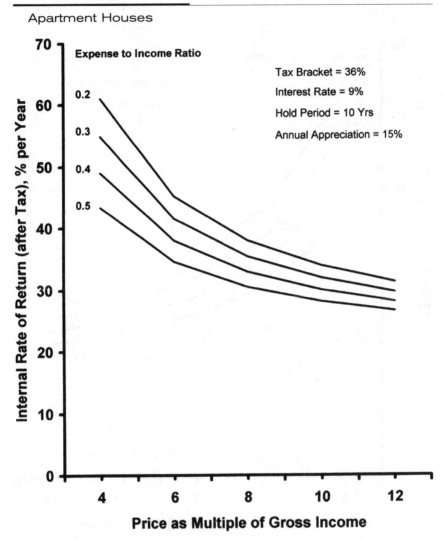

WORKSHEET 7-20

Apartment Houses

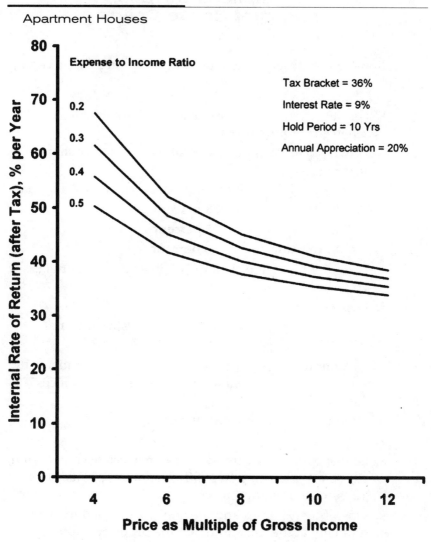

Assumptions Used for
Apartment House Charts

The following assumptions were used in compiling the preceding graphs:

1. Fees incurred at purchase (legal, escrow, loan fee): **2 percent of purchase price.**
2. Down payment at purchase: **20 percent of purchase price.**
3. Purchase price distribution for depreciation calculations:

   Building: **78 percent**

   Lot: **17 percent**

   Furnishings: **5 percent**
4. Period of mortgage or purchase installment contract: **25 years.**
5. Depreciation:

   Building: **27.5-year life, straight line**

   Furnishings: **7-year life**

   Improvements are included in expenses and are assumed to be equal to depreciation allowances each year.
6. Hold period prior to sale: **10 years.**
7. Terms at sale: **cash.**
8. Selling expenses incurred at sale (real estate commission, excise tax, recording fees, title insurance, points, etc.): 10 **percent of selling price.**
9. Operating expenses and income are assumed to increase annually at the same rate that the property appreciates in value.
10. Capital gains tax 20 percent. *Note:* It is recognized that capital gains tax rates are subject to change from those in effect at this writing. Refer to Appendix C for the effect of alternate capital gains tax rates.

CHAPTER 8

Tenants

Following the purchase of rental property, the primary tasks are tenant selection and property management. Most tenants fall into one of several basic categories.

TENANT TYPES

Type 1: Temporary Assignment Tenants These are tenants who will be located in the area for a limited time, perhaps one to two years. Corporate transfers, college exchange professors, and service personnel are typical examples. Usually stable and reliable, they will take good care of the property and make rental payments on time. They would probably purchase their own home if they were staying in the area.

Type 2: Young Marrieds or Families Young married couples or families who are still getting their feet on the ground financially make up this group. They are usually potential home buyers but may be several years away from such a purchase. The chances are good that they will be desirable tenants in terms of property care, although their job situation may be somewhat unstable.

Type 3: Interim Renters These are potential home owners who are interested in a rental situation for a limited period of time. They may have sold their home recently and be in the process of having a new one built, or they may be newcomers to the area. Typically, they are accustomed to and prefer rental houses to apartments, and they frequently have a large amount of household furnishings from their previous home that would not be adequately accommodated by an apartment. They are usually stable financially, but their primary interest is to locate and purchase a home of their own as soon as possible. They will probably take a limited interest in the house they're renting since it is an interim situation, and they are likely to move as soon as the lease expires.

Type 4: Perennial Renters This large group consists of individuals who are geared to renting. They are either unconvinced of the benefits of home ownership or cannot qualify for the loan requirements. While there are some excellent tenants in this category, they're a mixed bag; some may be less likely to provide good financial stability and can be marginal tenants in terms of property care. Therefore, this group needs careful screening.

Type 5: Adult Singles with Children Widowed, divorced, or otherwise single parents with children represent a relatively high-risk category. Although there are many good tenants in this group, the tenant's ability to provide adequate care for the property, particularly the grounds, can be a concern. This is because it is difficult for a single parent to work, keep house, and raise children. Again, careful screening is important to determine that the prospective tenant is fully prepared to accept this responsibility and to make adequate arrangements for such care. One solution is that the landlord take responsibility for maintenance and adjust the rent upward for rendering this service.

Type 6: Roommates or Group Singles Several single working adults or college students who live together on a temporary basis can be high-risk tenants, largely due to the lack of permanency that often characterizes these relationships. Please note that we are speaking in generalities. It is possible to have excellent tenants in this category. However, the potential exists for property neglect, damage, behavioral patterns objectionable to neighbors, and the possibility that the tenants might vacate the premises without proper notice.

If group singles are accepted, each should individually sign the lease agreement as well as a written statement precluding substitutions without your approval. An alternative is to have one of the individuals sign the lease agreement and be fully responsible on behalf of the group for fulfilling the terms of the lease.

BASIC OBJECTIVES

As can be seen in the brief outline of tenant types, some are preferable to others. The relative desirability of various types can be summarized by evaluating each in terms of three basic objectives or criteria regarding tenant selection:

Long-Term Occupancy   It is desirable to avoid frequent tenant changes. Each time a tenant vacates the house, rental income is lost, cleanup costs are incurred, and considerable time and money must be invested in advertising and in interviewing prospective tenants. An important objective is therefore to minimize tenant turnover.

Good Care of the Property   Tenants are wanted who will take good care of both the building and the grounds.

Financial Responsibility and Stability   It is important to select tenants who are likely to fulfill their financial obligations and meet rental payments on time. It costs time and money to evict tenants, and it can be a frustrating responsibility to deal with those who are lax or simply unable to fulfill financial obligations because of unemployment or other personal circumstances. It saves a lot of grief to have tenants who are on a sound financial footing.

Figure 8-1 summarizes the relative compatibility of each of the previously described tenant types in terms of three basic landlord objectives. This chart makes it clear that the first two types—Temporary Assignment tenants and Young Marrieds and Families—are likely to yield satisfactory tenants. The Adult Singles with Children type, and Roommates or Group Singles, represent high-risk categories that require thorough screening. The types labeled Interim Renters and Perennial House Renters are worthy of consideration although they also represent greater risk.

F I G U R E   8–1

House Tenant Types versus Objectives

Tenant Types	Objectives Regarding Tenants		
	Long-Term Occupancy	Good Care of Property	Financial Responsibility and Stability
Temporary Assignments	Fair	●	●
Young Marrieds/ Families	●	●	Fair
Interim Renters	Poor	Fair	●
Perennial House Renters	●	Fair	●
Adult Singles with Children	Fair	Poor	Poor
Roommates or Group Singles	Poor	Poor	Poor

● Good   ▓ Poor   ⟋ Fair

SCREENING TENANTS

A systematic screening system is essential to maximize prospects for getting desirable tenants. In order to do this, a tenant selection checklist should be used. This written list of requirements for tenants is aimed at determining the type of prospective tenant involved and helps identify high-risk categories where extra care in screening is important. It also provides other important selection information. The requirements on this checklist should be fair and reasonable; nondiscriminatory in terms of race, creed, color, or sex; and in writing. In fact, the checklist can be in the form of an application or questionnaire.

Figure 8-2 is a typical questionnaire that should be presented to prospective tenants at the time of the interview. Ask prospective tenants to complete and return it by mail, with the promise that they will be given a definite answer within a few days, and no more than a week, following receipt of the completed questionnaire. This approach relieves you of the uncomfortable position of having to reject prospective tenants at the time of the interview. It also permits you to compare several applications and to check out references before making a selection.

Typical items that should be covered in your tenant checklist include:

1. Minimum salary requirements

2. Evidence of steady employment

3. References

4. Pets

5. Number of occupants

6. Terms and deposits

Let's consider each of these items more thoroughly:

1. *Minimum Salary Requirements.* If you want stable tenants, make sure they can afford the rent. A good rule of thumb is that the tenants should earn about two and a half times the amount of the rent per month. In other words, if the house rents for $1500 per month, the prospective tenant should earn about $3800 per month.

2. *Evidence of Steady Employment.* Good tenants usually have stable jobs. Candidates should be eliminated who have had steady employment for less than a year, unless there is a good reason. This does not preclude individuals who have recently started a new job with another company, provided there is evidence of reasonable stability in previous employment. The intent is to avoid unstable job-hoppers who have a history of frequent employment changes, periods of unemployment, and location changes.

3. *References.* Always ask for references from previous landlords, and take the time to call and check them out. Most landlords are quite candid. Banking references also have some value. Possession of checking and savings accounts does not ensure that the party will be a good tenant, but such possession is a favorable indicator of financial responsibility and stability. The absence of either would be unusual and might signal a potential problem. For example, the absence of a checking account might be due to a bad check problem.

FIGURE 8-2

Prospective Tenant Questionnaire

Name _____ Phone _____

Legal Status: Single ☐   Married ☐   Divorced ☐   Widowed ☐

Social Security Number _____

Drivers License Number _____ State _____

Auto Model and Year _____ License No. _____ State _____

Persons to Occupy Premises: Relationship

_____   _____

_____   _____

_____   _____

Present Address _____

How Long at This Address? _____

Landlord or Agent _____ Phone _____

Previous Address _____

How Long at This Address? _____

Landlord or Agent _____ Phone _____

Present Employer _____ How Long _____

Address _____ Phone _____

Occupation _____ Monthly Gross Income _____

Previous Employer _____ How Long _____

Address _____ Phone _____

Occupation _____ Monthly Gross Income _____

Pets Owned: No ☐ Yes ☐ If yes, describe: _____

Name of Bank _____ Branch _____

Address _____

Type of Account: Checking ☐   Savings ☐

Name of Relative or Reference _____

Address _____ Phone _____

Estimated Length of Occupancy _____

Have you ever filed a petition in bankruptcy? Yes ☐ No ☐

Have you ever been evicted from a tenancy? Yes ☐ No ☐

I declare that the foregoing information is true under penalty of perjury and I agree that the landlord
may terminate any lease-rental agreement entered if any of the above information is untrue.

Signature of Applicant _____

Date _____

4. *Pets.* Pets are nice, but they can inflict damage to the property. Large dogs in particular can demolish shrubbery and lawns, particularly if they are kept fenced in the backyard all day. Dogs kept indoors frequently damage the carpets or chew things, and in some instances leave a permeating odor that is difficult to remove after the tenants move out unless the carpets and drapes are thoroughly cleaned or replaced. A good general rule is to limit the pets to cats or small dogs or, better yet, to exclude them entirely. In any case, increase the security deposit required if pets are involved, in order to cover the increased damage potential.

5. *Number of Occupants.* The number of tenants should be appropriately matched to the size of the house. A house that is crowded with more people than it can comfortably accommodate will sustain undue wear and tear. You can use your own judgment in this regard, but a limit based upon two persons per bedroom is a good general rule. For example, six persons should be about the limit for a three-bedroom home.

6. *Terms and Deposits.* Typical terms call for the payment of the first and last months' rent in advance, with succeeding monthly rental payments due at the start of each month. In addition, an initial deposit should be made by the tenant at the time the lease agreement is signed in order to hold the property until the balance of the money owed is paid. This deposit should be about half the first month's rent, assuming the tenant plans to take occupancy of the premises within a week or two. In the event that the prospective tenant changes his or her mind and backs out of the deal, he or she loses this deposit. It protects the landlord from the potential loss of income that would occur as a result of taking the house off the market.

There should also be a security deposit to cover the cost of repairing possible damage to the property during the tenant's occupancy. It can also be used to cover cleaning costs in the event that the tenant fails to clean up adequately after vacating the house, though there could be a separate cleaning deposit as well. The security deposit is returned to the tenant provided the property is left in good condition and in the same state of cleanliness that existed at the time the tenant moved in. Otherwise, appropriate deductions are made to cover the required repairs or work. For residential properties, a security deposit of one month's rent is quite common.

In order to avoid possible misunderstandings, it is essential to inspect the premises with the tenant prior to occupancy and to fill out a form that describes its condition in some detail. Figure 8-3 may be used for this purpose. The landlord and the prospective tenant carefully

FIGURE 8–3

Description of Property Condition

Address of Property _____

Tenant (Lessee) _____ Owner (Leaser) _____

A checkmark (X) indicates that the item in question is clean, in good condition, and/or properly maintained immediately prior to occupancy by the tenant. Use the space to describe any exceptions.

KITCHEN

Walls _____	Windows _____	Sink _____
Ceiling _____	Light Fixtures _____	Cupboards _____
Doors _____	Refrigerator _____	Counters _____
Floor _____	Stove _____	Other _____

MAIN BATHROOM

Walls _____	Windows _____	Toilet _____
Ceiling _____	Light Fixtures _____	Medicine Cabinet _____
Door _____	Tub/Shower _____	Counter/Cabinet _____
Floor _____	Sink _____	Other _____

2nd BATHROOM

Walls _____	Window _____	Toilet _____
Ceiling _____	Light Fixtures _____	Medicine Cabinet _____
Door _____	Tub/Shower _____	Counter/Cabinet _____
Floor _____	Sink _____	Other _____

LIVING ROOM

Walls _____	Drapes _____	Light Fixtures _____
Ceiling _____	Floors/Carpets _____	Other _____
Doors _____	Windows _____	_____

HALLWAY(S)

Walls _____	Floor/Carpet _____	Other _____
Ceiling _____	Electrical Fixtures _____	_____

MASTER BEDROOM

Walls _____	Windows _____	Closet _____
Ceiling _____	Light Fixtures _____	Other _____
Door _____	Curtains/Drapes _____	_____

2nd BEDROOM (Middle-Sized)

Walls _____	Windows _____	Closet _____
Ceiling _____	Light Fixtures _____	Other _____
Door _____	Curtains/Drapes _____	_____

3rd BEDROOM (Smallest)

Walls _____	Windows _____	Closet _____
Ceiling _____	Light Fixtures _____	Other _____
Door _____	Curtains/Drapes _____	_____

GARAGE

Car Door _____	Other Door _____	Other _____

GROUNDS/YARDS

Front Lawn Mowed/Trimmed _____	Shrub Areas Weeded _____
Back Lawn Mowed/Trimmed _____	Other _____

Other Comments on General Condition of Property: _____
_____

The undersigned tenant hereby acknowledges that the property described by this form was inspected by the tenant immediately prior to occupancy and that the condition of said property was as indicated herein.

Signature of Tenant _____ Date _____

check each room together and note on this form any existing damage or problem. A similar form is filled out when the tenant vacates the premises, thereby providing a formal record of repairs, cleanup, or yard maintenance work that needs to be taken care of or paid for out of the security deposit before a refund is made. Such a procedure will motivate the tenant to take better care of the property.

Land

Land investment differs from income property with regard to both the typical cash flow pattern and the terms influencing profitability.

CASH FLOW PROFILE

In contrast to income property, land investment is characterized by a larger negative cash flow during the hold period relative to the total investment. This is due to the absence of rental income generated and because land is not depreciable. In fact, there is no cash inflow generated during the hold period to offset installment payments and carrying costs. Accordingly, it typically takes more capital to carry a land investment than an apartment building or rental house of comparable value. You will recall that rental houses may also produce a negative cash flow pattern during the hold period, although less than that of land, while apartment buildings may be expected to yield a positive cash flow.

Figure 9-1 illustrates the annual before-tax cash flow pattern for land purchased for $50,000 under terms consisting of 20 percent down and a 10-year installment contract at 8 percent interest. The illustration also assumes that the land is sold after five years for cash at a price of $100,570, reflecting a growth rate of about 15 percent per year. In addition, Figure 9-1 makes representative assumptions for

FIGURE 9-1

Annual Cash Flow Before Tax, Typical Land Investment

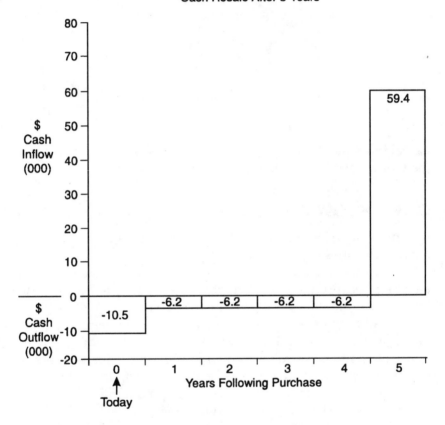

ASSUMPTIONS
Purchase Price: $50,000
Down Payment: 20%
Interest Rate: 8%
Appreciation Rate: 15%
Cash Resale After 5 Years

property tax payments as well as other expenses associated with purchase and resale transactions.

Note that a large cash outflow is incurred at the time of purchase due to the down payment and purchase expenses. The annual cash outflows during the ensuing four years are constant and consist of contract or mortgage installment payments and property tax payments. The cash inflow at sale (fifth year) is attributable to the net income received from the sale of the property after paying off the balance owed on the purchase contract, the sales commission, legal costs, and other miscellaneous expenses related to the sale.

Figure 9-2 presents the cash flow for the same example on a cumulative basis. Note that by the fourth year the cumulative cash outflow has grown to over $35,000, illustrating the substantial

FIGURE 9-2

Cumulative Cash Flow Before Tax, Typical Land Investment

ASSUMPTIONS
Purchase Price: $50,000
Down Payment: 20%
Interest Rate: 8%
Appreciation Rate: 15%
Cash Resale After 5 Years

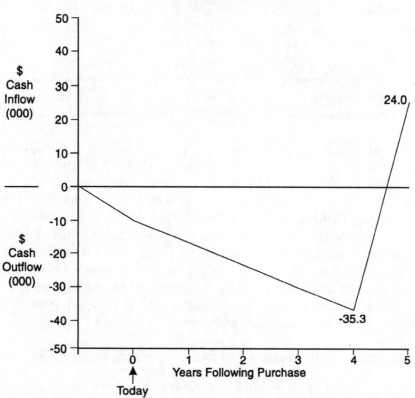

cash drain attributable to carrying costs during the hold period and emphasizing how important it is for the investor to be in a sufficiently strong financial position to accommodate these costs. The large cash inflow at sale at the end of the fifth year produces a cumulative net gain of about $24,000 and results in an average annual rate of return on investment of about 16 percent before taxes.

PROFITABILITY UNDER VARIOUS CASH SCENARIOS

The profitability of land investments is influenced by three types of variables. The first has to do with the *inherent growth characteristics* of the property, rather than the terms under which it is purchased or sold. More specifically, these are the hold period, the appreciation rate, and the cash-out period following sale. The second set of variables consist of the negotiable terms under which the property is purchased—the *buy terms*. These include down payment, contract period, and interest rate for the purchase contract. The third set of variables are the *sell terms*, which consist of the down payment, contract period, and interest rate for the installment contract under which the property is sold. Of course, if the property is sold for cash, these last three variables are not applicable. While most of these terms are self-explanatory, a few warrant further explanation.

Inherent Growth Characteristics   The *hold period* refers to the number of years the property is held by the investor after purchase until it is sold. *Appreciation rate,* as in the case of income property, refers to the average annual percent increase in value that the investor expects to occur during this hold period. The *cash-out period* applies only if the property is sold on an installment basis rather than for cash. It is the number of years following the sale until the contract is fully paid off. This reflects the fact that property sold under an installment contract is frequently paid off prior to expiration of the full contract term. All of these inherent growth characteristics variables are judgment calls that the investor must make at the time of purchase.

Buy Terms   This second set of variables are those over which the investor has more direct control since they can be influenced through negotiation. *Down payment,* of course, is the percentage of purchase price paid in cash at the time of purchase. *Contract period* refers to the number of years over which the balance owed on the purchase contract is to be paid. *Interest rate* is the rate charged under terms of the purchase contract.

Sell Terms   These are similar to the buy terms except they apply to the installment contract under which the property is sold following the hold period. Ideally, the investor would like to sell the property for cash rather than under installment terms, in which case these sell terms would not apply.

KEY INFLUENCES ON PROFITABILITY

If the investor sells land on an installment basis rather than for cash, the expected rate of return tends to diminish. Figure 9-3 illustrates this for a typical land investment in which the property is purchased under an installment contract and sold five years later under similar installment terms.

Both the buy and sell terms are assumed to call for 20 percent down, 10-year contract periods, and 9 percent interest. Separate curves are plotted for different rates of appreciation. Note that the rate of return on invested capital tends to diminish as the period from sale to cash-out increases. This emphasizes the importance of investing in land that is relatively close to end-use application, providing good prospects for cash sale or at least early cash-out if sold on an installment basis.

Appreciation rate is the most significant single influence on profitability. Figure 9-4 illustrates how the return on invested capital increases with appreciation rate for two typical land investment scenarios. The assumptions for the buy and sell terms and other variables are summarized on the chart.

Other variables in the profitability equation—hold period, down payment, interest rate, and contract period—are also worth serious attention but exert much less influence on profitability than appreciation rate and the potential for cash sale or early cash-out. There are exceptions to this, of course, when it does make sense to invest in land even though it may be quite a few years away from end use. These situations, however, are usually those which provide the potential for value-building opportunities, discussed later in this chapter.

FIGURE 9-3

Land Investment: Impact of Deferred Cash-Out on Profitability

ASSUMPTIONS
Hold Period: 5 Years
Buy Terms:
    Down payment: 20%
    Contract Period: 10 Years
    Contract Interest Period: 9%

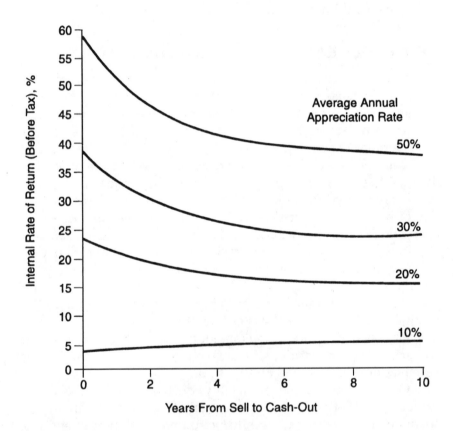

SCREENING FOR PROFITABILITY

The worksheet chart series at the end of this chapter provides the before-tax rates of return calculated for different combinations of variables concerning inherent growth characteristics, buy terms, and sell terms. The assumptions reflected in the calculations are

F I G U R E   9–4

Land Investment: Impact of Appreciation Rate on Profitability

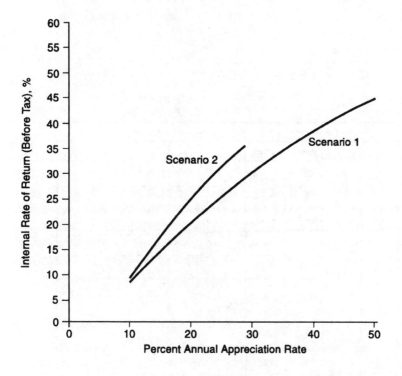

ASSUMPTIONS	Scenario 1	Scenario 2
Hold Period:	5 yrs.	7 yrs.
Period From Sell to Cash-Out:	2 yrs.	——
Buy & Sell Terms:		
Down Payment:	20%	Cash Sale
Interest Rate:	6%	——
Contract Period:	10 yrs.	——

explained following the charts. While still a preliminary screening tool, they do provide rate-of-return values for a wide range of variables. These include both the buy and sell negotiable terms (percent down payment, contract period, and interest rate), as well as combinations of the inherent growth characteristics variables (hold period, years to cash-out after resale, and annual appreciation rate). This worksheet chart series should be used when you have sufficient information to realistically input such a broad range of variables.

In situations where the investigation concerning a prospective land investment has not progressed to the point where it is realistically possible to realistically input the negotiable terms likely to apply, as called for in the worksheet series at the end of the chapter, the Figure 9-5 chart series, which follows, is provided. They are useful as a quick test or screening to determine whether more thorough investigation and analysis appear warranted. They test whether the prospective investment is likely to fall within an acceptable profitability range based on the anticipated inherent growth characteristics alone (hold period, years from sell to cash-out, and annual appreciation rate).

FIGURE 9–5A

Land Investment Screening Chart

				▨ MOST PROBABLE RANGE			
				▨ LESS PROBABLE RANGE			

GROWTH CHARACTERISTICS				PROBABLE RETURN ON INVESTED CAPITAL				
		APPRECIATION RATE		BELOW 11%	11% TO 20%	21% TO 30%	31% TO 50%	OVER 50%
YEARS FROM BUY TO SELL	YEARS FROM SELL TO CASH-OUT	% ANNUAL RATE OF GROWTH	SALES PRICE RELATIVE TO PURCHASE PRICE	NOT ACCEPT-ABLE	MARGINAL	GOOD	EXCELLENT	OUT-STANDING
1	0 (CASH SALE)	20	1.2	▨				
		30	1.3				▨	
		50	1.5					▨
	2	20	1.2	▨	▨			
		30	1.3		▨	▨		
		50	1.5				▨	▨
	5	20	1.2	▨	▨			
		30	1.3		▨	▨		
		50	1.5			▨	▨	
	10	20	1.2	▨	▨			
		30	1.3		▨	▨		
		50	1.5		▨	▨	▨	

FIGURE 9–5B

Land Investment Screening Chart

Legend: ▨ = MOST PROBABLE RANGE ░ = LESS PROBABLE RANGE

GROWTH CHARACTERISTICS				PROBABLE RETURN ON INVESTED CAPITAL				
		APPRECIATION RATE		BELOW 11%	11% TO 20%	21% TO 30%	31% TO 50%	OVER 50%
YEARS FROM BUY TO SELL	YEARS FROM SELL TO CASH-OUT	% ANNUAL RATE OF GROWTH	SALES PRICE RELATIVE TO PURCHASE PRICE	NOT ACCEPTABLE	MARGINAL	GOOD	EXCELLENT	OUT-STANDING
2	0 (CASH SALE)	10	1.2	▨				
		20	1.4		▨	░		
		30	1.7				▨	░
		50	2.3					▨
	2	10	1.2	▨				
		20	1.4		░	▨	░	
		30	1.7			░	▨	
		50	2.3				░▨░	
	5	10	1.2	▨				
		20	1.4		▨			
		30	1.7		░	▨		
		50	2.3			░	▨	
	10	10	1.2	▨				
		20	1.4		▨	░		
		30	1.7		▨	░		
		50	2.3			░	▨	

Built into the charts is the presumption that most land will be bought and sold on an installment contract basis involving down payments ranging from 10 to 30 percent of the sales price. The charts also assume that the interest rates involved in such transactions will be about the same at both the buy and sell ends of the investment scenario and will not exert a major influence on profitability outcome. Prospective investments that pass this initial screening should, of course, be analyzed in greater depth using the worksheet charts at the end of this chapter, as well as more definitive internal rate-of-return analysis based on a detailed projection of cash flow.

FIGURE 9–5C

Land Investment Screening Chart

	MOST PROBABLE RANGE
	LESS PROBABLE RANGE

GROWTH CHARACTERISTICS				PROBABLE RETURN ON INVESTED CAPITAL				
		APPRECIATION RATE		BELOW 11%	11% TO 20%	21% TO 30%	31% TO 50%	OVER 50%
YEARS FROM BUY TO SELL	YEARS FROM SELL TO CASH-OUT	% ANNUAL RATE OF GROWTH	SALES PRICE RELATIVE TO PURCHASE PRICE	NOT ACCEPT-ABLE	MARGINAL	GOOD	EXCELLENT	OUT-STANDING
3	0 (CASH SALE)	10	1.3	▨				
		20	1.7			▨	░	
		30	2.2				▨	░
		50	3.4					▨
	2	10	1.3	▨				
		20	1.7		▨	░		
		30	2.2			▨	░	
		50	3.4				▨	░
	5	10	1.3	▨				
		20	1.7		▨	░		
		30	2.2			▨	░	
		50	3.4			░	▨	░
	10	10	1.3	▨				
		20	1.7		▨	░		
		30	2.2		░	▨	░	
		50	3.4			░	▨	

In using the Figure 9-5 series, the variables are listed on the left-hand portion of the chart:

Years from buy to sell: the hold period.

Years from sell to cash-out: the anticipated number of years from the time the investor resells to the time full payment of the balance due is received.

Appreciation rate: the rate at which the land appreciates in value. This is indicated in two ways in the Figure 9-5 series for your convenience. One approach is to express appreciation rate in terms of an annual growth rate. This is the percent the land increases in

FIGURE 9–5D

Land Investment Screening Chart

Legend:
- ▨ MOST PROBABLE RANGE
- ░ LESS PROBABLE RANGE

YEARS FROM BUY TO SELL	YEARS FROM SELL TO CASH-OUT	APPRECIATION RATE — % ANNUAL RATE OF GROWTH	APPRECIATION RATE — SALES PRICE RELATIVE TO PURCHASE PRICE	BELOW 11% — NOT ACCEPTABLE	11% TO 20% — MARGINAL	21% TO 30% — GOOD	31% TO 50% — EXCELLENT	OVER 50% — OUTSTANDING
5	0 (CASH SALE)	10	1.6	▨				
		20	2.5			▨		
		30	3.7				▨	
		50	7.6					▨
	2	10	1.6	▨				
		20	2.5			▨		
		30	3.7			░	▨	
		50	7.6				▨	
	5	10	1.6	▨				
		20	2.5		▨			
		30	3.7			▨		
		50	7.6				▨	
	10	10	1.6	▨				
		20	2.5		▨			
		30	3.7			▨		
		50	7.6				▨	

value each year over the preceding year. It is an average annual compound rate of growth. Another way of expressing growth is to estimate its sale price as a factor of purchase price. For example, if land is purchased for $10,000 and is sold after two years for $23,000, it would have increased by a factor of 2.3:

$$\frac{\$23{,}000 \text{ (Sale Price)}}{\$10{,}000 \text{ (Purchase Price)}} = 2.3$$

Or, the sale price is 2.3 times the original purchase price. As noted by Figure 9-5B, land that is held for two years and increases by a

FIGURE 9–5E

Land Investment Screening Chart

		MOST PROBABLE RANGE
		LESS PROBABLE RANGE

GROWTH CHARACTERISTICS				PROBABLE RETURN ON INVESTED CAPITAL				
		APPRECIATION RATE		BELOW 11%	11% TO 20%	21% TO 30%	31% TO 50%	OVER 50%
YEARS FROM BUY TO SELL	YEARS FROM SELL TO CASH-OUT	% ANNUAL RATE OF GROWTH	SALES PRICE RELATIVE TO PURCHASE PRICE	NOT ACCEPTABLE	MARGINAL	GOOD	EXCELLENT	OUT-STANDING
	0 (CASH SALE)	10	2.0	▨				
		20	3.6			▨		
		30	6.3				▨	
7	2	10	2.0	▨				
		20	3.6		▨			
		30	6.3			▨		
	5	10	2.0	▨				
		20	3.6		▨			
		30	6.3			▨		
	10	10	2.0	▨				
		20	3.6		▨			
		30	6.3		▨			

factor of 2.3 actually grows at a rate of 50 percent per year. You may use either of the ways described above to express appreciation rate, depending upon which you feel most comfortable with.

For all three of the basic variables used to describe the investment in the Figure 9-5 series, only selected values are listed. Where the expected value for a given variable falls somewhere between the values listed, the reader must interpolate the result by examining the profitability indicated for the values listed that most closely approximate and that bracket the particular value desired. The

FIGURE 9–5F

Land Investment Screening Chart

MOST PROBABLE RANGE
LESS PROBABLE RANGE

GROWTH CHARACTERISTICS				PROBABLE RETURN ON INVESTED CAPITAL				
		APPRECIATION RATE		BELOW 11%	11% TO 20%	21% TO 30%	31% TO 50%	OVER 50%
YEARS FROM BUY TO SELL	YEARS FROM SELL TO CASH-OUT	% ANNUAL RATE OF GROWTH	SALES PRICE RELATIVE TO PURCHASE PRICE	NOT ACCEPT-ABLE	MARGINAL	GOOD	EXCELLENT	OUT-STANDING
10	0 (CASH SALE)	10	2.6	▨				
		20	6.2			▨		
		30	13.8				▨	
	2	10	2.6	▨				
		20	6.2		▨			
		30	13.8				▨	
	5	10	2.6	▨				
		20	6.2		▨			
		30	13.8			▨		
15	0 (CASH SALE)	10	4.2	▨				
		20	15.4		▨			
	5	10	4.2	▨				
		20	15.4		▨			

range of values indicated are more than adequate to accomplish the intended purpose of an initial screening.

The right-hand portion of the Figure 9-5 series lists various ranges of expected profitability expressed as an average annual rate of return on invested capital. The type of shading used indicates the range of profitability most likely to occur for the various combinations of the variables listed on the left-hand part of the chart. Determination of the profitability ranges that might be expected is based upon an extensive computer analysis encompassing thousands of selected scenarios. These scenarios reflect a wide range of negotiable terms and include representative allowances for costs involved in the typical buy and sell transactions, such as sales commission, property taxes, and closing costs. The reason that a fairly wide range of profitability outcomes is possible is because a wide range of possibilities exist for the negotiable variables that are not included in the charts. These include the terms of down payment, interest rate, and contract period for both the buy and sell transactions. The results indicated do assume, as mentioned before, that the leverage principle is applied in all cases concerning the purchase transaction, and that the down payment falls somewhere between 10 and 30 percent of the purchase price. Similarly, it has been assumed that in cases other than cash sales, the land would be sold on installment contracts involving down payments also in the range of 10 to 30 percent.

It must be emphasized that the results indicated are not precise assessments of profitability. No guarantee is intended that all possible transactions will conform to the ranges suggested by the Figure 9-5 series. The charts do provide a good guideline reference, however, concerning the most likely profitability bracket for land with the selected growth characteristics indicated, based upon a massive body of analytical effort encompassing a wide spectrum of typical transactions.

Investments that have a profitability outlook of less than 20 percent return per year on invested capital are considered unacceptable or marginal. Obviously, if the investment represents a very stable low-risk situation, a rate of return that falls below 20 percent may well be considered attractive. These are judgments that you the investor must make on an individual basis.

You will note that the profitability charts for land investment are on a before-tax rather than after-tax basis, as was the case for rental houses and apartments. This reflects the fact that tax shelter benefits are more significant for income property, due largely to the deductibility of depreciation expense from taxable income. Further, the combinations of buy and sell terms for land are much more varied than for income properties since land is more often sold, as well as purchased, under installment terms. Because of this added complexity and the significance factor, the before-tax approach was felt to be appropriate.

FACTORS CAUSING LAND VALUES TO RISE

Because of the importance of investing in land that offers the potential for high rates of appreciation, the investor should be alert to the underlying factors influencing such an outcome. Three basic factors cause land to increase in value:

1. Inflation
2. Economic Pressure that Precipitates Development
3. Value Building

Inflation

Inflation causes prices to escalate but does not produce real gain. Land is a helpful hedge against inflation, but inflationary increases alone may not produce real gain, particularly if the interest rate paid on the installment contract under which the property is purchased offsets inflationary price increases. Exceptions occur during periods in which inflation rates escalate periodically to successively higher levels, while the investor holds a fixed interest purchase contract. In addition, the tax benefits enjoyed by debtors, as discussed in Chapter 2, are a positive factor. Nevertheless, dependency upon inflation alone as the basis for value increase is not a good investment strategy and usually fails to produce an acceptable rate of return.

Economic Pressure that Precipitates Development

Another factor that causes land to appreciate is economic pressure that precipitates land development. This is the single most important requirement to successful land investment. Economic growth in an area produces jobs; jobs attract people; and a growing population creates pressures for housing and an array of supporting business and commercial services, all of which require land. Land in this environment typically increases in value at a rate substantially higher than the rate of inflation, providing the basis for real gain. If this is your strategy for profitable land investment, the key is selection—first, of a good growth area, and then of a good site within this area. If done effectively, the economic forces in action will cause the property to increase in value at a rate that produces a good return. The basic principle emphasized earlier—buying only land that has the potential of maturing to end-use application within a relatively short time—is extremely important under this investment approach.

Value Building

The remaining factors that cause land values to rise are *improvement, subdivision,* and *use upgrade.* These three factors all involve value-building techniques and are effective strategies in certain situations.

Improvement   It is sometimes possible to improve raw land at very little expense through superficial changes that make it more marketable. Most prospective buyers have difficulty envisioning the true potential of a site that is covered, for example, with undergrowth, dense thicket, and trees. A few hours with a bulldozer to open up unpaved access paths or roads or to clear out portions of the property in order to improve visibility for prospective buyers will usually enhance its appeal considerably. Experienced contractors and developers do not have difficulty envisioning the potential of property covered with foliage and dense thicket. However, if the primary market consists of potential home owners who are interested in developing the site with the house of their dreams, they need some help in getting a better perspective of the land being offered.

The bulldozer should be used to fill gullies, cut roads, clear openings for potential building sites, and pile up rubbish for burning or hauling away. No attempt should be made to change contours or grades on large tracts, however, since this becomes very expensive and should be reserved for the developer or builder to perform. Your purpose is simply to make the land more attractive and easier to show and to help the prospective buyer visualize his or her future dream house comfortably nestled among the trees on this attractive building site.

More extensive improvement actions are also possible, such as drilling a well to provide water or building more elaborate roadways (other than bulldozer-cleared dirt access paths). But this type of improvement usually becomes quite expensive and should be avoided by all but the most experienced investors. Otherwise there is a tendency to end up investing too much front-end money that could be used more effectively in other leveraged investments.

Subdivision   This is the second strategy for value building. It involves buying a relatively large tract and subdividing it into several smaller parcels. In most cases, subdivision by the nonprofessional land investor should be limited to what does not require extensive surveys and platting. It is necessary to check out local laws to determine constraints in this regard, but many counties permit the owner to subdivide land into several smaller parcels without surveys or extensive approval procedures. The aggregate value of subdivided parcels would likely be substantially higher than that of the entire tract as a single parcel. This is the "buy wholesale, sell retail" concept. It also provides expanded market potential since there are many more potential buyers for 2- to 5-acre sites than for 20-acre tracts. Further, most potential buyers for large tracts are investors rather than end-users. By subdividing, it is not only possible to charge a higher per acre price, but the property becomes oriented toward the end-user market (rather than the investor market) in which purchasers are generally cash buyers. This would not be true for very large parcels of land, such as a 100-acre tract that is subdivided into four 25-acre tracts. The resale market would still be oriented largely toward investors rather than end-users, and the potential for cash sale would remain relatively low. However, an increase in the per acre value would be achieved.

Use Upgrade   Another strategy for value-building is use upgrade. This involves actions to make the land suitable for a more valuable use. This usually means rezoning. Land has certain economic value based upon its intended use. Zoning is the device used by local governments to regulate the character of property and implement a comprehensive plan for orderly community development. This is, of course, both necessary and desirable, and its proper and legitimate use serves the public interest. However, zoning is neither infallible nor unchangeable, and herein lies the potential for significant investment opportunities. Comprehensive plans and related zoning patterns are based on the judgment and forecasting ability of agencies charged with this responsibility. But the projection of community development patterns and needs is a complex process that is done imperfectly, at best, because of many variables that cannot always be accurately anticipated. As a result, long-range comprehensive plans and related zoning regulations are not static. They must be revised and modified periodically to accommodate unanticipated growth patterns and needs of the community, and this fact provides opportunities to the astute investor.

Zoning Changes and Variances

There are at least two rezone strategies. The first involves anticipating potential changes in current zoning based on development patterns—buying property in the path of such anticipated change and then waiting for progress to do its thing. The main problem with this approach is the difficulty in predicting the timing of such change. Unless one has unusual foresight or advance information regarding possible commercial or industrial development plans, a long hold period may be involved. By the time such changes become general knowledge, property values will have escalated to reflect this fact. This means it is necessary to recognize potential high-growth areas or future development plans that are not yet in the take-off phase and to move ahead of the market. This is particularly difficult to do for land. At the very least, it means becoming thoroughly familiar with the locality and keeping abreast of all development plans.

Similar opportunities exist in rental house investments, perhaps with slightly better predictability and less risk. The gradual takeover of residential areas peripherally located to the downtown business districts of many metropolitan areas illustrates the potential opportunities in this regard. Basic land economics sometimes dictate the expansion of commercial or business areas and the demolition of adjacent residential housing, particularly if it is somewhat old and antiquated. Such residential housing may therefore provide good investment opportunities, with the potential for substantial increase in value through rezoning. The risk is somewhat lower than for land investments since housing can be rented during the interim. In the event that the anticipated expansion of business and commercial areas does not occur and rezoning opportunities fail to materialize, rental houses still offer the prospect of good profitability. This is due to the favorable rental income that a house convenient to the downtown location usually provides, and through the capital gain achieved at resale, assuming at least moderate rates of appreciation.

A second approach to capitalizing on potential rezoning opportunities is to buy property on a contingency basis that is believed to be ripe for a zoning change. In other words, enter into a contractual agreement with the seller to buy property but make the sale contingent upon approval of an appeal for rezone of the property. This approach requires recognizing signs that signal changing uses in an area. As areas develop over time, changes occur that make zoning plans obsolete. Visualize what is needed in today's environment that was not needed when the area was zoned; by so doing, you may be able to find a valid reason for requesting a change in zoning or a variance. More specifically, this strategy involves the following approach:

1. Concentrate in a specific area and become an informed specialist.
2. Study the current land-use plan and zoning, which should be accessible to the public.
3. Obtain copies of the zoning for specific areas of interest.
4. Study recent actions concerning this area to understand zoning changes, revisions, and variances that have been approved.
5. Look for trends or changes in development patterns for business and residential areas and try to identify sites that are zoned incorrectly.
6. Find the names of lawyers who have a good track record in getting changes approved.

After locating a potential rezoning opportunity, the next step is to present a request for a change or variance. Such a request is usually made at a meeting of the zoning board or an equivalent agency designated to hear such appeals. In order to be successful, the request must be based upon sound logic and a well-prepared presentation. A good way to become knowledgeable about how to proceed is to sit in on actual zoning board meetings when zoning requests are being considered. This will not only help you understand how such appeals are made, but will provide you with knowledge about the board members and their attitudes toward various reasons for rezoning.

The objective of the application for such change is to win the zoning board over to your viewpoint. It is therefore essential to view the request from their perspective and to address the problem in terms of their interests rather than your own. Emphasize why the proposed change is in the best interests of the community involved and demonstrate that it would not be harmful to others. Support this position with well-prepared evidence and visual aids for diagrams, layouts, statistics, and other supportive information pertinent to the case. Remember that the board is predisposed against any change. In order to alter this attitude, they must understand the logic and arguments for change. If they do not understand all of the issues and ramifications, they will likely vote to preserve the status quo, particularly if it is unclear that the change is to the best interests of all parties. It may be desirable to employ a competent attorney to present the appeal. A lawyer is not emotionally involved in the proposed change and may therefore do a better job in objectively presenting the case.

In some situations, a variance may be more feasible than a zoning change. A variance is generally used to provide relief to the property owner when strict application of the ordinance will deny the owner beneficial use of his or her property. For example, consider a house in close proximity to a commercial development. A case might be made that the house is not marketable at a reasonable price as a residence, making it unattractive to prospective home buyers. Similarly, a vacant lot may not be suitable for the type of building or application called for by zoning regulations because of its size or shape. In order to succeed in such an appeal, it is usually necessary to demonstrate that the unnecessary hardship involved is unique to the owner's particular property and is not self-created, and that if forced to comply with the ordinance, the owner will be unable to realize a reasonable return or make reasonable use of his or her property. Further, a variance will normally be granted only if the proposed use change does not change the essential character of the neighborhood or zoning district in which it is located and, in addition, does not detrimentally impact adjacent property or the interests of the community in general.

SUMMARY

To summarize, here are some of the more important guidelines to successful land investment:

1. Land that appreciates in value at a rate of 15 to 20 percent per year will usually yield a satisfactory rate of return provided it is held for at least three years and sold for either cash or near-cash terms (meaning the investor is fully paid off within two or three years of the sale).

2. Land that appreciates in value at the rate of 20 to 30 percent per year or more will almost always yield a satisfactory result, unless it is both held for an unusually short period of time (a year or less) and sold under installment terms that defer investor-cash-out for several years.

3. Land should generally be purchased under leveraged terms; the preceding guidelines (items 1 and 2) are based on the general premise that down payment at purchase does not exceed 30 percent.

4. In addition to appreciation rate, price and down payment are the factors that exert the greatest influence on profitability. These are considerably more important than interest rate or contract period.

5. In general, it is best to buy land that is within five years of end-use application. End-use application refers to the type of development for which the property will ultimately be used. For example, the end-use application of raw land may be residential houses, commercial buildings, industrial developments, recreational areas, and so on. The reason for this is that cash is seldom paid for land except by the end-user. If the property is sold on an installment basis rather than for cash, the result is usually a significantly lower profit rate.

6. Become a regional specialist. Assuming a favorable economic outlook for the area, become familiar with local values and detailed development plans that will affect these values. In order to become sufficiently familiar with an area, the scope of your geographical interest should be

limited. Become knowledgeable about current zoning, ownership of major property blocks, current land values and recent sales prices, highway and road development plans, industrial and housing development plans, and other information relevant to the selection and assessment of good properties in the area.

7. Be alert for value-building opportunities. Land that has good growth potential by virtue of location and local area economic trends is further enhanced if it lends itself to subdivision, rezoning opportunities, or low-cost improvements.

Chart Section

Land
Profitability Analysis Charts

Worksheet—Land

This worksheet form may be used for each prospective investment to summarize the data required to use the charts that follow, as well as to compile input data needed for a more detailed profitability and cash flow analysis to be performed by the real estate firm or financial advisor of your choice. Permission is granted to make copies of the form.

Worksheet Information—Land

Property Identification: _____

Data for Using the Charts:

1. Buy terms:

    a) Down payment (10%, 20%, or 30%) _____

    b) Loan period (10 or 15 years) _____

    c) Interest rate (6% or 9%, whichever is closer)_____

2. Estimated hold period (3 or 5 years) _____

3. Estimated annual appreciation rate (10%, 20%, or 30%) _____

4. Probable sell terms:

    a) Down payment (15%, 20%, 30%, or Cash Sale) _____

    b) Loan period (10 or 15 years) _____

    c) Interest rate (6% or 9%)_____

Additional Data for Detailed Profitability and Cash Flow Analysis:

5. Buy terms:

    a) Down payment (%)_____

    b) Loan period (years)_____

    c) Interest rate (%) _____

6. Sell terms:

    a) Down payment (%)_____

    b) Loan period (years)_____

    c) Interest rate (%) _____

7. Annual property taxes ($)_____

8. Years from sell to cash-out _____

9. Purchase fees (% of price or $)_____

10. Selling expense at time of sale (% of selling price)_____

11. Year and amount of any balloon payments under the
    purchase contract_____

WORKSHEET 9–1

Internal Rate of Return (%) (Before Tax)—Land Investment

Cash Resale Scenarios

Buy Terms	Percent Down	Contract Period (Yrs)	Interest Rate (%)	Hold Period - Years to Resale								
				3			5			10		
				Appreciation Rate (%)								
				10	20	30	10	20	30	10	20	30
	10	10	6	2	36	57	8	30	45	10	24	35
			9	*	28	52	2	26	42	7	22	33
		15	6	2	38	60	9	33	48	10	25	37
			9	*	30	55	1	28	45	7	23	35
	20	10	6	3	28	46	8	26	40	9	22	33
			9	*	24	42	3	23	38	7	21	32
		15	6	3	30	48	8	28	42	10	24	34
			9	*	24	44	3	24	39	7	22	33
	30	10	6	4	24	39	8	24	36	9	21	31
			9	*	21	37	4	21	34	8	20	30
		15	6	4	25	40	8	25	37	9	22	32
			9	*	21	38	4	22	35	7	21	31

*Negative Return

WORKSHEET 9-2

Internal Rate of Return (%) (Before Tax)—Land Investment

Scenario:
Hold Period (Yrs. to Resale) 3
Years to Cash Out After Resale 2
Annual Appreciation Rate (%) 10

	Percent Down	Contract Period (Yrs)	Interest Rate (%)	Sell Terms					
				Down Payment (%)					
				15		20		30	
				Contract Period (Years)					
				10		10		10	
				Interest Rate (%)					
Buy Terms				6	9	6	9	6	9
	10	10	6	4	8	4	8	4	8
			9	*	*	*	*	*	*
		15	6	4	9	4	9	3	8
			9	*	*	*	*	*	*
	20	10	6	5	8	5	8	4	7
			9	*	2	*	2	*	1
		15	6	4	8	4	8	4	8
			9	*	1	*	1	*	*
	30	10	6	5	7	5	7	5	7
			9	1	4	0	3	*	3
		15	6	5	8	5	7	5	7
			9	*	3	*	3	*	2

*Negative Return

WORKSHEET 9-3

Internal Rate of Return (%) (Before Tax)—Land Investment

Scenario:
Hold Period (Yrs. to Resale)   3
Years to Cash Out After Resale   2
Annual Appreciation Rate (%)   20

Buy Terms				Sell Terms					
				Down Payment (%)					
				15		20		30	
				Contract Period (Years)					
				10		10		10	
Percent Down	Contract Period (Yrs)	Interest Rate (%)		Interest Rate (%)					
				6	9	6	9	6	9
10	10	6		21	24	22	25	24	27
		9		15	18	16	19	18	21
	15	6		23	26	24	28	28	30
		9		16	20	17	21	19	23
20	10	6		18	20	19	21	20	22
		9		14	17	15	17	16	18
	15	6		19	22	20	23	22	24
		9		15	17	15	18	16	19
30	10	6		16	18	17	19	18	20
		9		13	16	14	16	14	17
	15	6		17	19	18	20	19	21
		9		14	16	14	16	15	17

*Negative Return

WORKSHEET 9-4

Internal Rate of Return (%) (Before Tax)—Land Investment

Scenario:
Hold Period (Yrs. to Resale)   3
Years to Cash Out After Resale   2
Annual Appreciation Rate (%)   30

Buy Terms				Sell Terms					
				Down Payment (%)					
				15		20		30	
				Contract Period (Years)					
				10		10		10	
	Percent Down	Contract Period (Yrs)	Interest Rate (%)	Interest Rate (%)					
				6	9	6	9	6	9
	10	10	6	33	35	34	37	38	40
			9	28	31	30	32	33	36
		15	6	36	38	38	40	42	44
			9	31	33	32	35	36	39
	20	10	6	28	30	29	31	32	34
			9	25	27	26	28	28	30
		15	6	30	32	31	33	34	36
			9	26	29	27	30	30	32
	30	10	6	25	27	26	28	28	29
			9	23	25	24	25	25	27
		15	6	26	28	27	29	29	31
			9	24	25	24	26	26	28

*Negative Return

WORKSHEET 9-5

Internal Rate of Return (%) (Before Tax)—Land Investment

Scenario:
Hold Period (Yrs. to Resale)   3
Years to Cash Out After Resale   5
Annual Appreciation Rate (%)   10

				Sell Terms					
				Down Payment (%)					
				15		20		30	
				Contract Period (Years)					
				10		10		10	
Percent Down	Contract Period (Yrs)	Interest Rate (%)		Interest Rate (%)					
				6	9	6	9	6	9
10	10	6		5	10	5	10	5	10
		9		*	4	*	4	*	2
	15	6		5	11	4	11	3	12
		9		*	2	*	1	*	*
20	10	6		5	9	5	9	5	9
		9		0	5	*	4	*	4
	15	6		5	10	5	10	4	10
		9		*	4	*	3	*	1
30	10	6		5	9	5	9	5	8
		9		2	5	1	5	1	5
	15	6		5	9	5	9	5	9
		9		0	5	*	4	*	3

*Negative Return

WORKSHEET 9-6

Internal Rate of Return (%) (Before Tax)—Land Investment

Scenario:
Hold Period (Yrs. to Resale) 3
Years to Cash Out After Resale 5
Annual Appreciation Rate (%) 20

				Sell Terms					
				Down Payment (%)					
				15		20		30	
				Contract Period (Years)					
				10		10		10	
Percent Down	Contract Period (Yrs)	Interest Rate (%)		Interest Rate (%)					
				6	9	6	9	6	9
10	10	6		15	19	16	20	19	23
		9		11	15	11	16	13	17
	15	6		18	22	19	24	23	27
		9		11	17	12	17	14	20
20	10	6		14	17	15	18	16	19
		9		10	14	11	14	12	15
	15	6		15	19	16	20	19	22
		9		11	15	11	16	13	17
30	10	6		13	16	13	16	15	17
		9		10	13	11	14	11	14
	15	6		14	17	14	18	16	19
		9		10	14	11	14	12	15

Buy Terms (row group label)

*Negative Return

WORKSHEET 9-7

Internal Rate of Return (%) (Before Tax)—Land Investment

Scenario:
Hold Period (Yrs. to Resale) 3
Years to Cash Out After Resale 5
Annual Appreciation Rate (%) 30

Buy Terms

Percent Down	Contract Period (Yrs)	Interest Rate (%)	Sell Terms					
			Down Payment (%)					
			15		20		30	
			Contract Period (Years)					
			10		10		10	
			Interest Rate (%)					
			6	9	6	9	6	9
10	10	6	24	27	26	29	30	33
		9	20	24	21	25	25	28
	15	6	27	31	30	33	35	38
		9	22	26	24	28	29	33
20	10	6	21	24	22	25	25	28
		9	18	22	19	22	22	25
	15	6	23	26	25	28	28	31
		9	20	23	21	24	24	27
30	10	6	19	22	20	23	22	25
		9	17	20	18	21	20	22
	15	6	15	23	22	24	24	27
		9	18	21	19	22	21	24

*Negative Return

WORKSHEET 9-8

Internal Rate of Return (%) (Before Tax)—Land Investment

Scenario:
Hold Period (Yrs. to Resale)   5
Years to Cash Out After Resale   2
Annual Appreciation Rate (%)   10

Buy Terms				Sell Terms					
				Down Payment (%)					
				15		20		30	
				Contract Period (Years)					
				10		10		10	
				Interest Rate (%)					
	Percent Down	Contract Period (Yrs)	Interest Rate (%)	6	9	6	9	6	9
	10	10	6	7	9	8	9	8	9
			9	3	5	3	5	2	4
		15	6	8	10	8	10	8	10
			9	1	4	1	4	0	3
	20	10	6	7	9	7	9	7	9
			9	4	6	4	5	3	5
		15	6	7	9	8	9	8	9
			9	3	5	3	5	2	4
	30	10	6	7	9	7	9	7	9
			9	4	6	4	6	4	6
		15	6	7	9	7	9	7	9
			9	4	6	4	5	4	5

*Negative Return

WORKSHEET 9–9

Internal Rate of Return (%) (Before Tax)—Land Investment

Scenario:
Hold Period (Yrs. to Resale) 5
Years to Cash Out After Resale 2
Annual Appreciation Rate (%) 20

Buy Terms				Sell Terms					
				Down Payment (%)					
				15		20		30	
				Contract Period (Years)					
				10		10		10	
Percent Down	Contract Period (Yrs)	Interest Rate (%)	Interest Rate (%)	6	9	6	9	6	9
10	10	6		21	23	22	23	23	24
		9		18	20	19	20	19	21
	15	6		23	25	24	26	26	27
		9		19	21	20	22	21	23
20	10	6		19	21	20	21	21	30
		9		17	18	17	19	18	19
	15	6		21	22	21	23	22	23
		9		18	19	18	20	19	20
30	10	6		18	19	18	19	19	20
		9		16	17	16	18	17	18
	15	6		19	20	19	20	20	21
		9		17	18	17	18	18	19

*Negative Return

WORKSHEET 9-10

Internal Rate of Return (%) (Before Tax)—Land Investment

Scenario:
Hold Period (Yrs. to Resale)　　5
Years to Cash Out After Resale　2
Annual Appreciation Rate (%)　30

Buy Terms	Percent Down	Contract Period (Yrs)	Interest Rate (%)	Sell Terms					
				Down Payment (%)					
				15		20		30	
				Contract Period (Years)					
				10		10		10	
				Interest Rate (%)					
				6	9	6	9	6	9
	10	10	6	32	33	33	34	34	36
			9	29	31	30	31	32	33
		15	6	34	36	35	37	37	39
			9	31	33	32	34	34	35
	20	10	6	29	30	30	31	31	32
			9	27	28	28	29	29	30
		15	6	31	32	31	32	33	34
			9	28	30	29	30	30	31
	30	10	6	27	28	27	28	28	29
			9	25	26	26	27	27	28
		15	6	28	29	28	30	30	31
			9	26	27	27	28	28	29

*Negative Return

WORKSHEET 9–11

Internal Rate of Return (%) (Before Tax)—Land Investment

Scenario:
Hold Period (Yrs. to Resale)   5
Years to Cash Out After Resale   5
Annual Appreciation Rate (%)   10

Buy Terms				Sell Terms					
						Down Payment (%)			
				15		20		30	
				Contract Period (Years)					
				10		10		10	
Percent Down	Contract Period (Yrs)		Interest Rate (%)	Interest Rate (%)					
				6	9	6	9	6	9
10	10		6	7	10	7	10	7	10
			9	3	6	3	6	3	6
	15		6	7	11	7	11	8	11
			9	1	5	1	5	*	4
20	10		6	7	9	7	9	7	9
			9	4	7	4	6	4	6
	15		6	7	10	7	10	7	10
			9	3	6	3	6	2	5
30	10		6	7	9	7	9	7	9
			9	5	7	5	7	4	7
	15		6	7	9	7	9	7	9
			9	4	6	4	6	3	6

*Negative Return

WORKSHEET 9-12

Internal Rate of Return (%) (Before Tax)—Land Investment

Scenario:
Hold Period (Yrs. to Resale)   5
Years to Cash Out After Resale   5
Annual Appreciation Rate (%)   20

				Sell Terms					
				Down Payment (%)					
				15		20		30	
				Contract Period (Years)					
				10		10		10	
Percent Down	Contract Period (Yrs)	Interest Rate (%)		Interest Rate (%)					
				6	9	6	9	6	9
10	10		6	17	19	17	20	19	21
			9	14	17	15	17	16	18
	15		6	19	22	20	22	22	24
			9	15	18	16	19	17	20
20	10		6	16	18	16	18	17	19
			9	14	16	14	16	15	17
	15		6	17	19	18	20	19	21
			9	14	17	15	17	16	18
30	10		6	15	17	15	17	16	18
			9	13	15	14	15	14	16
	15		6	16	18	16	18	17	19
			9	14	16	14	16	15	17

Buy Terms (row label)

*Negative Return

WORKSHEET 9-13

Internal Rate of Return (%) (Before Tax)—Land Investment

Scenario:
Hold Period (Yrs. to Resale) 5
Years to Cash Out After Resale 5
Annual Appreciation Rate (%) 30

			Sell Terms					
Buy Terms			Down Payment (%)					
			15		20		30	
			Contract Period (Years)					
			10		10		10	
			Interest Rate (%)					
Percent Down	Contract Period (Yrs)	Interest Rate (%)	6	9	6	9	6	9
10	10	6	25	27	26	28	29	30
		9	23	25	24	26	26	28
	15	6	28	30	29	31	32	34
		9	25	27	26	28	29	31
20	10	6	23	25	24	26	26	28
		9	21	23	22	24	24	26
	15	6	25	27	26	28	28	30
		9	23	25	24	26	26	28
30	10	6	22	24	22	24	24	26
		9	20	22	21	23	23	24
	15	6	23	25	24	26	26	27
		9	21	23	22	24	24	25

*Negative Return

Assumptions Used for Land Investment Charts

The following assumptions were used in compiling the preceding charts:

1. Fees incurred at purchase (legal, escrow, loan fee): **1.0 percent of purchase price.**
2. Property taxes: **0.5 percent of purchase price annually.**
3. Fees incurred upon selling the property (real estate, legal, title insurance, etc.): **11 percent of sale price.**

CHAPTER 10

Negotiating the Deal

Negotiating is an important part of buying and selling real estate, or any other product or service for that matter. Substantial amounts of money can be made or lost in a very short period of time based upon how well this aspect of the investment activity is conducted. In addition to some *basic principles* that should be kept in mind, several specific *tactics* are described in this chapter. Even if a real estate agent is the negotiator on your behalf, you will still be involved in the negotiating process through the terms offered and tactics employed.

BASIC PRINCIPLES

Principle 1: Maximize Your Knowledge Position before Negotiating Specific Terms

Knowledge is power. You need knowledge about the other party, about the property in question, and about the terms and conditions that will yield a profitable result. This means adequate prenegotiation research concerning property values and other factors that influence the terms necessary to produce a profitable result. The charts in this book will help you in this regard.

Since information concerning the other party's circumstances and motivations for selling is important but often difficult to obtain, enter discussions in an alert and listening mode. Avoid intellectual pride, don't try to demonstrate your mental agility, and don't hesitate to ask "dumb" questions. Encourage the other party to do much of the talking, and listen for clues that provide insights into the circumstances: the pressures causing the purchase or sale, his or her deadlines, financial motivations (whether the need is for cash, income, tax protection, or long-term gain), and other relevant information. People are influenced by biases and prejudices that stem from a variety of experiences and circumstances. Investors who recognize the human equation and tailor their negotiating strategy to accommodate the unique peculiarities and perspectives of the other party—who in fact is your opponent in the negotiating game—are likely to fare far better than those who do not.

Beyond understanding your opponent, knowledge about the property is essential. You should know its market value based upon comparable properties available in the area. Although you may not be seriously interested in other properties, if you lead the other party to believe there are viable alternatives, you may have an advantage. In addition to market value, it is essential to know the price and terms that make the property economically attractive. This is the basis for establishing the limits of acceptable compromise and structuring an effective give-and-take strategy.

Principle 2: Don't Set Your Initial Demands Too Near Your Final Objective, and Probe for the Bottom Line

Within a range of acceptability in terms of probable profitability potential, the primary objective in negotiating is to achieve the best possible price and terms. Since it is impossible to be certain how far your opponent will retreat from his or her initial position, it is important to open with terms that are substantially more favorable to you than those you are ultimately willing to accept. Most real estate agents advise their clients to set the asking price at a level that provides a negotiating cushion. It is easier to sell the property if the agent can recommend a counteroffer to the buyer that is slightly below the asking price and that the agent knows the seller will accept. The buyer has virtually nothing to lose by offering a significantly reduced price from the one being asked. The buyer can always come back with a revised offer, and in the meantime has probably punctured the opponent's aspiration level. At the very least, it should elicit a response that provides better insight as to the true bounds of the seller's expectations.

If you are embarrassed about doing this face-to-face, use an intermediary such as the real estate agent. However, do not take the real estate agent into your confidence as to whether you are serious about this counteroffer or whether it is a tactic to test your opponent. Any salesperson on a commission is understandably influenced by self-interest. If you allow the real estate agent to believe you are serious, he or she will do his or her best to influence the seller to give serious consideration to your offer. This approach can of course be carried to extremes with detrimental results, particularly if you are the seller. It is possible to discourage potential buyers if the property is excessively overpriced; few real estate agents will devote substantial effort to showing and selling such property.

Principle 3: Raise Your Aspiration Level and Deflate Your Opponent's

Aspiration level refers to expectations. Studies reveal that people who aim high achieve better results. This is why motivational or success seminars typically focus on setting goals and building self-confidence to achieve them. Aspiration levels and goal-setting in real estate investment begin with profit expectations. Profitability objectives provide the basis for the specific terms that must be achieved in the negotiating process and should help avoid wasting time in marginal situations where the buyer and seller are too far apart. A real estate agent who understands your requirements will be more selective about the properties he or she presents to you. If you are willing to settle for less, you will be treated accordingly. High targets or goals may result in more deadlocks, but in the long run you will negotiate more attractive terms from your position.

In addition to raising your aspiration level, you want to deflate your opponent's. Aspiration levels in real estate tend to be fragile and unstable. Home owners typically put their houses on the market at initial prices that exceed true market value. This reflects strong personal attachment and the good care and hard work that have been put into the house over the years. This expectation level wilts, however, after the house has been on the market for several weeks without serious offers. A progressive deflation of the asking price typically follows a declining aspiration level. It is important to recognize that your opponent has such expectations, and that part of the negotiating strategy should be to gracefully deflate them. If you are the buyer, an obvious approach is to suggest a substantially lower price than the one being asked. Other approaches include a lukewarm attitude, calling attention to defects, commenting on deficiencies, or making the other party aware of competitive offerings you are considering.

If you are the seller, the objective is to deflate the other party's expectations. You may preempt a price-squeeze attempt by informing the other party that you have rejected prior offers below your asking price or by stating your intent to increase the price in the future. Real estate agents often use this approach, informing potential house buyers that the next block of homes in the development tract will be at higher prices due to increasing costs. The potential buyer not only loses any hope that the seller might accept a lower price, but feels pressured to move quickly to avoid the penalty of a price increase. Another approach is to suggest that other potential buyers are also considering the property and that its availability cannot be assured apart from an earnest agreement. In any case, the basic intent is to preempt an undesirable counteroffer, rather than waiting for such an offer to be made and then rejecting it. No one likes to be rejected or to lose face.

Principle 4: Negotiate the Most Critical Items First and Concentrate on Those Issues That Exert the Greatest Leverage on Profitability

It is easy to fall into the trap of dwelling on secondary issues that are not critical to maximizing potential profitability. Assuming that financing arrangements relative to down payment, contract period, and interest rate are generally in line with prevailing practice, the primary negotiable term is price. If an acceptable price cannot be negotiated, don't waste a lot of time on other issues. Beyond price, it is important to maximize leverage. Concentrate on reducing the down payment, negotiating deferred payments, and extending the contract period to minimize carrying costs. Focusing attention on and limiting initial discussion to such primary issues will save a lot of time and indirectly work to your advantage concerning secondary issues, as well. After the major obstacles are successfully hurdled, parties tend to become more committed to successfully consummating the transaction, and secondary issues fall into place more readily.

Principle 5: Employ a Conservative Concession Policy

Be stingy in your concession policy! Most of us have been instilled with the concept of fair play since childhood and feel obligated to reciprocate in some way if our opponent makes a concession. This is a nice philosophy, but it has no place in negotiating. Negotiating is not synonymous with sportsmanship; it doesn't have to be fair. Forget about tit for tat, splitting the difference, and all the other clichés reflecting the attitude that mutual compromise automatically means an acceptable result. Remember that an acceptable result is dictated solely by achieving or exceeding terms compatible with the profitability objective or criteria you have established. A good policy is to not make the first concession, to not reciprocate on concessions made by the other party unless it is unavoidable, to make the other party work for every concession they receive, and to get something for everything you give. Keep in mind that negotiations are not for the purpose of building lasting friendships. This is not to suggest you should do anything unethical, but that you should avoid the tendency to put negotiations on the same plane as day-to-day interfaces with business associates in which there is an ongoing or continuing relationship and where it may be appropriate at times to compromise for the sake of future harmony.

If at all possible, it is usually advantageous to take the initiative in the basic offer. This tends to establish a reference point around which concessions are made. By the same token, avoid allowing the other party to use this approach. In the event that he or she makes a counteroffer that substantially deviates from your terms, do not give dignity to such an offer or allow it to become a baseline reference against which compromises are subsequently negotiated.

Principle 6: Never Accept a Significant Counteroffer or Proposal without Analysis

Quickie negotiations can be disastrous—unless you are prepared and the other party is not. During the course of negotiations, it is probable that the other party will present counterproposals involving terms that you have not considered or carefully thought through but that strike a responsive chord and sound plausible. In such cases, receive the offer courteously, ask as many questions as necessary to ensure a thorough understanding, and then adjourn the meeting to permit the necessary time to consider and thoroughly digest the proposal and its ramifications apart from the pressures of a negotiating environment. Avoid expressing or telegraphing a reaction, either positive or negative, but rather, receive the proposal impassively, with the assurance that you will give it careful consideration and respond subsequent to review.

It is normally impossible to fully understand all of the implications of an unexpected proposal. The first reaction may be superficial and totally misleading. Remember, the party who proposes an unexpected set of conditions has a knowledge advantage over the other.

For the very reason that quickie negotiations can be disastrous to the unprepared party, this approach is an effective tactic provided you are on the giving rather than receiving end. A distinct advantage can be acquired by taking the initiative and proposing terms that careful analysis has revealed favor your position. That is why it is so helpful to perform the prenegotiation analysis thoroughly and to understand the boundaries of terms and conditions that are acceptable in the context of your overall profit objectives.

Principle 7: Use Intermediaries or Confederates When It Is to Your Advantage

An intermediary is simply a third party who acts as an agent or go-between for the two parties who are negotiating. In real estate, the intermediary is usually the real estate agent.

In general, it is wise to conduct the negotiations through an agent or intermediary if you are a novice and the other party is a pro, or if you are less experienced and less knowledgeable. Inexperienced negotiators are likely to telegraph their feelings to those with more experience. The use of an intermediary in these circumstances provides a buffer that provides time to think through and understand all of the ramifications of the offer or counteroffer. Much of the advantage enjoyed by a more experienced adversary can be nullified by taking the added time to think through, analyze, research, and seek counsel concerning proposals.

By the same token, if you are more experienced, more knowledgeable, and better prepared than the other party, it may well be to your advantage to negotiate on a personal basis, since the odds would then be in your favor.

The other aspect of third-party involvement has to do with the use of confederates or advisors. These are individuals who accompany you during the negotiations, perhaps to provide assistance and counsel or because they will have some type of ownership interest or involvement in the venture. Husband and wife teams are among the most common alliances in this regard, and a word is necessary about one of the most common errors made by couples in purchasing a home. Couples have a tendency to openly debate their reactions in the presence of the sales agent or seller. In viewing houses, husbands and wives should agree beforehand upon a course of conduct that will enhance their subsequent negotiating position rather than undermine it. This means that features of the house will be observed but restraint will be exercised in openly expressing favorable reactions. Further, the strategy should be to display and openly express concern over its undesirable characteristics and to call attention to potential problems. This lowers the seller's aspiration level and leaves the way open to focus upon price as the primary issue in subsequent negotiations.

Confederates or advisors may enhance your negotiating posture in several other ways. They provide psychological reinforcement by creating a two-on-one situation. More important, two heads are better than one and can uncover more knowledge about the other party and more insights concerning the property. Further, a confederate or advisor provides the opportunity for collaboration and reduces the risk of premature response to terms or proposals that have not been adequately analyzed.

Principle 8: Look For a Better Deal for Both Parties

There is a tendency to measure success in negotiations by the degree of suffering that can be inflicted upon the other party. A better measure of success is the degree to which terms are achieved that satisfy objectives, and it is frequently possible for both parties to achieve this result without one party or the other being penalized. The interests of both parties in the negotiating process are best served by consummating the transaction as quickly as possible under terms that are mutually acceptable or favorable. There is no unique formula for accomplishing this except to be alert to the other party's needs and receptive to innovative approaches that will mutually enhance the transaction for both parties.

For example, assume a potential buyer is found for a house you are selling, but the house needs repairs requiring a near-term cash outlay for which the buyer is not financially postured. The problem may be solved by a sales agreement conditional upon the necessary repairs and improvements being made by the seller at an increased sales price that equitably reflects these added costs. The buyer would avoid the near-term added cash outlay associated with such improvements, since they would be a part of the total sales price and financed through a long-term mortgage. The objectives of both parties would be satisfied; neither would benefit at the expense of the other.

Principle 9: Place the Burden of Proof or Satisfaction on the Other Party

You will gain a psychological advantage if the negotiating encounter is structured so the other party must attempt to convince you the transaction in question is an attractive opportunity. If you are the buyer, maintain sufficient interest to draw the seller into an active attempt to convince you of the virtues of the property he or she is selling. If you are a legitimate but hesitant prospect in the seller's eyes, he or she is likely to attempt to sweeten the offer sufficiently to escalate your interest to a more positive and enthusiastic level; it is usually easier to extract concessions under such circumstances.

If you are the seller, you must of course avoid being drawn into this type of relationship. Demonstrate a sincere interest and receptiveness to understanding the buyer's needs, and a willingness to explore ways to accommodate these needs, but do not be drawn into the position of pursuing the buyer with concessionary probes in the hope of determining an acceptable approach. To do so reveals the softness of your own position and tends to make the buyer suspicious about the transaction in general. Allow the buyer to initiate counteroffers in writing and with an earnest money commitment. By doing so, the buyer defines the level of potential interest and places you in a response mode, with the option to modify the proposals as appropriate.

TACTICS

There are hundreds of negotiation tactics, a few of which are particularly useful in real estate. An awareness of these tactics will not only strengthen your negotiating technique, but will enable you to recognize when they are being used against you.

The Standard Practice Tactic

This is one of the most powerful and commonly used tactics in real estate negotiations. In essence, it involves obtaining agreement from the other party to certain terms and conditions on the basis that such terms are widely accepted standard practice and therefore not subject to challenge or negotiation. We are conditioned to accept that rules, regulations, or terms that are printed on standard forms are authoritative, legitimate, and normal and that compliance is more or less automatic.

This power of the written word can be used as an effective tactic in many real estate transactions, the more common applications being the so-called standard forms dealing with earnest money agreements, lease agreements, agreements on property listings, and sales agreements between buyers and sellers. To employ the tactic, preprinted contracts that favor your position are required. If you own an apartment or rental house, you should acquire preprinted lease agreements designed primarily to protect the interests of the landlord. Such forms are available at many stationery stores, or you may draw up your own and have it printed. By using a well-designed form, it is possible to eliminate much discussion concerning the terms of the lease that you feel are important.

The Bogey Tactic

Bogey means phantom, specter, or ghost. In other words, a bogey is something that usually exists only in the mind of the party who believes in its existence. In the bogey tactic, a third party bogey becomes the "bad guy." To understand how it works, assume that an investor locates a parcel of land for sale under terms involving a

$10,000 down payment. The investor likes the property but does not wish to invest that amount of front-end cash. He or she may say, "I really like the property, but I only have $7500 in cash." The bogey or bad guy in this case is the cash limitation. Because the buyer has indicated a sincere desire for the property and has agreed with the seller concerning its excellence, the seller is likely to respond in a positive manner and try to accommodate this limitation.

Japanese nationals use the bogey tactic with great skill in international transactions. In transactions involving governmental approval, for example, the bogey is typically the minister of finance or some other high governmental official. The negotiating team will often demonstrate real interest and very positive attitudes concerning a potential transaction, and they skillfully align themselves with the opponent in exploring ways to overcome the limitations imposed by their bogey. American businesspeople tend to swallow this ploy and transfer their hostility from the negotiating team itself to this unseen authority. The negotiating team members are regarded as fine fellows who must operate under the difficult constraints of an independent authority, and the sellers typically find themselves working in close cooperation with the opposing team in exploring compromise solutions that usually equate to a gradual shift in terms favoring the other side.

The countermeasure to the bogey tactic is to determine the level of authority of the party with whom you are dealing in the negotiating process. Don't allow the other party to draw you into a prolonged investment of time before they introduce the bogey. Determine whether the party has the authority to agree to terms reached through negotiation, and if not, who does have such authority. In addition, determine at the outset what other constraints or limitations may exist concerning the other party's ability to consummate the transaction.

The Good Guy/Bad Guy Tactic

This is similar to the bogey tactic in that it involves a third party, but with a slightly different twist. Instead of introducing a real or imaginary obstacle that must be overcome, a bad guy is used to undermine the opponent's aspiration level through strong demands that will make the opponent more receptive to a less-demanding position presented later on. For example, one partner might initially take a particularly strong stand. His or her reserved associate would stay largely on the sidelines during this phase. When a deadlock occurs, the reserved associate takes over with a more concessionary attitude. The contrast makes the more moderate demands of this second individual seem quite reasonable, even though they may represent a substantial departure from the original goals or aspiration level of the party against whom the tactic is employed. To illustrate, envision two partners negotiating with the seller for a parcel of land for sale at $50,000, 20 percent down, and 10 percent interest with contract payments over 10 years. The dominant or spokesman partner (bad guy) might bluntly indicate that all the property was worth and all that he would consider paying was $35,000, 10 percent down, and 8 percent interest—an offer the seller would likely reject. A few days later the passive partner (good guy) might make a personal call to the seller and in a much more conciliatory tone indicate a desire for the property, an understanding of the seller's position, and a desire to negotiate. But the best he could probably get his partner (bad guy) to agree to would be $45,000, 12 percent down, and 9 percent interest. The seller might find this more generous offer acceptable.

The Deadline Tactic

Deadlines serve several useful purposes and should be placed on all offers made. Their primary purpose is to apply pressure on the other party to react to proposals. If you are a buyer, a deadline on your offer communicates to the seller that you probably intend to pursue other properties or explore other alternatives if the pending transaction falls through. This places the seller at risk for losing the sale. If you are the seller, it communicates to the potential buyer that you intend to actively attempt to sell the property to other parties.

Deadlines are also useful because they provide protection against being drawn into protracted holding patterns in which time works against you. The longer you are kept on the hook, the greater the susceptibility to unfavorable compromises due to the sunk investment in time and effort. Deadlines put a time limit on uncertainty and force clarification of the other party's intent.

If you are on the receiving end of a deadline, on the other hand, recognize it for what it usually is: a pressure tactic designed to achieve a response. The general response to deadlines should therefore be to ignore them. While there is always some risk to this approach, it will usually work to your advantage. Ignoring deadlines usually amounts to calling the other party's bluff and communicating that you will not be pressured into unattractive terms or a premature commitment where important issues or questions have not yet been satisfactorily resolved.

The Nibbling Tactic

"Nibbling" involves extracting additional minor concessions after basic agreement has been achieved on the major terms. The reason that nibbling often works well following general agreement on major issues is because of the psychological commitment to the transaction. When final agreement is so close, most people are reluctant to jeopardize consummation for the sake of a few additional concessions that are relatively inconsequential. You can take advantage of this tendency and sweeten up most deals during the final phases of the negotiation. For example, in the case of a land purchase, you might "nibble" for balloon or deferred payments in place of uniform monthly installment payments. This should be done after agreement is reached on such basic terms as price, interest rate, contract period, and down payment. Or you might nibble for a reduced down payment or lower interest rate, provided agreement has been achieved on the other basic terms. In the case of a house purchase, you might nibble for the inclusion of a number of minor repairs to the house at the owner's expense or for the inclusion of appliances, draperies, and other extras that might normally be available but at additional cost.

In the event that the other party is doing the nibbling, you can employ several countermeasures. One, obviously, is outright rejection. Remember, after many hours of negotiation and being on the verge of mutual agreement, the other party is probably just as committed to consummating the transaction as you are and is unlikely to walk away from the deal simply because he or she is unable to squeeze out a few extras. A better approach, however, is to deflate the other party's aspiration level with respect to further concessions before they ask for them. This can be done by escalating your demands or by indicating second thoughts regarding concessions you previously yielded.

The Tie-Up Tactic

This is a buyer's tactic in which property is tied up or essentially removed from the market under an agreement that conveys intent to purchase but is contingent upon certain conditions. In reality, this is what most earnest agreements represent. It is possible to structure these agreements so the buyer has a variety of "outs." For example, the agreement may be contingent on obtaining satisfactory financing (which the buyer determines). Or it may be contingent on prior sale of other property owned by the buyer, on approval of certain zoning changes, on approval by appropriate governmental agencies of development plans, on approval by the buyer's architect, on soil test analysis and suitability, or on any number of other contingencies structured into the agreement. Tying up the property through such an agreement may take it off the market during a period when it is most marketable. It also places the property under the control of the buyer at virtually no cost or risk, because the potential buyer pays no interest on the value of the property and no installment payments during this holding action. Even if the buyer ultimately purchases the property under the terms defined by the agreement, he or she has achieved some cash flow benefit for the period during which the property has been tied up.

CHAPTER 11

Group Investments or Joint Ownership

There are several reasons for considering teaming up with other individuals or participating in some kind of a group or joint ownership arrangement. Perhaps the primary reason for such arrangements is the pooling of resources, although there are several other potential benefits as well.

BENEFITS

Better Opportunities and Price   Investors with limited funds are usually faced with limited investment opportunities. The more funds you have at your disposal, the greater the selection and range of investment opportunities available. In the case of land, a greater funding capability permits the purchase of larger parcels at lower prices and provides the opportunity to increase the value through subdivision. In the case of rental properties, a group investment approach may permit the purchase of a larger and more modern apartment complex than would be possible on an independent basis, providing a more favorable investment situation. A larger complex usually provides more income per dollar of price than a smaller complex, as well as a lower ratio of operating expenses to gross income, particularly if it is a more modern structure.

Better Diversification and Risk Dissemination   Even though you may have the financial capability to handle one or more real estate investments independently, it may be advantageous to diversify your real estate investment portfolio by owning shares in a greater number of properties than would be possible on a go-it-alone basis. Most well-selected real estate investments provide the expectation of good profitability, but there is no assurance that every investment will be successful. Unpredictable events will likely cause some to fare less favorably than others. By investing in a larger number of properties, you spread the risk instead of putting all of your eggs in one basket, reducing exposure to serious loss in the event that an investment turns sour.

Professional Management   For investors who do not have the time or inclination to manage their own property, certain types of group investments may have appeal. Some of the more common types are outlined below. If the group investment approach is pursued, legal counsel is desirable. Laws are constantly changing, and the most suitable group investment arrangement will depend largely upon the type of property involved; the credentials, objectives, and capabilities of the participants; and prevailing tax laws and regulations governing various types of syndicated investments.

   The ensuing discussion on this subject is limited and intended only to provide broad conceptual familiarity. Areas of interest should be researched further and, as already suggested, specific investment opportunities reviewed with an attorney. Group investments can be like marriages: Ill-conceived unions can and often do lead to future misunderstandings, unexpected liability exposure, and expensive legal actions among participants.

LIMITED PARTNERSHIPS

These have been a popular form of group investment. They are commonly used by builders and developers to raise investment capital for a real estate venture or for group purchase of land. There are two types of partners involved: the *general partner* and *limited partners.* The general partner manages and controls the investment, while the limited partners are owners. Limited partners are, in effect, silent partners whose ownership shares are proportionate to their investment. They have no vote or voice in decisions with respect to the venture. The limited partners' liability is normally limited to the amount of their contribution to the partnership capital. Since it is a form of partnership, the syndicate itself pays no income taxes. Instead, each of the partners pays income taxes on a pro rata share, determined on the basis of ownership.

A limited partnership is not perpetual, but exists for the ownership of a specific property and must have a specified termination date or event, such as sale of the property. There are restrictions concerning the transfer of partnership interest, and limited partners must not be active participants in its management. If they are, they may be considered general partners, subject to the liabilities of general partners. There are also requirements governing the qualifications of the general partner, such as the level of assets that must be owned relative to the net worth of the partnership.

Of extreme importance in limited partnerships is the competence and integrity of the general partner. If you invest in a limited partnership, insist on information concerning the track record of the firm or individuals who are the general partners. Be sure that the provisions of the agreement are reasonable in terms of front-end fees to cover such items as administrative costs, promotional expense, and sales expense (to sell ownership shares). Syndication firms tend to do a very good job of putting these deals together and selling limited partnership shares, but they frequently fail in the follow-through management and resale effort. This is particularly true if the arrangement for compensating the general partner is primarily front-end loaded, as is frequently the case.

A better remuneration arrangement is one that provides the general partner with motivation to carry the transaction to successful completion and profitable resale. This can be done by minimizing front-end compensation and, instead, providing remuneration on the basis of success achieved in terms of ultimate profitability. For example, the general partner might be compensated through a defined share of the profit. Some typical arrangements of this type provide for the payment of 15 to 20 percent of the net profit to the general partner, in addition to a front-end fee sufficient to cover syndication costs, as well as appropriate annual management fees throughout the hold period. These fees and charges are justified if equitably structured, since the general partner should be fairly compensated for the entrepreneurial effort involved in putting the deal together, negotiating both its purchase and sale, and providing overall management. Ongoing management functions include the preparation of financial reports, collection of installment payments from the limited partners, payment of taxes and purchase contract installment payments, and fulfillment of a variety of other related responsibilities.

Apart from participating as a limited partner, you might consider organizing a limited partnership in which you are the general partner, provided you are capable and willing to perform the responsibilities called for, as briefly outlined above. This can be an excellent way to join with several friends or associates in a real estate venture without relinquishing overall control of the management responsibility. In addition to maintaining such control, you would receive a share of the gain proportionate to your investment, plus additional remuneration for the services performed as general partner.

JOINT TENANCY

Under this form of joint ownership, each owner enjoys joint possession of the property. In other words, each owner has an individual interest in the whole property, rather than each owning a designated part of the whole. In joint tenancy, the undivided interest of the owners is with survivorship, which means that if one of the joint tenants dies, the property passes on to the remaining joint tenants, and the survivors hold title or claim to the property free from debts and claims against the deceased join tenant. Accordingly, joint tenancy property cannot be disposed of in a will. The term *tenant*, incidentally, is a bit confusing and does not refer to tenants in the tenant/landlord sense, but rather to the joint owners. In joint tenancy ownership, a joint tenant is personally liable for all expenses incurred on the property. In order for a joint tenancy to stand up in court, it is necessary to demonstrate that the joint owners have equal interests at the same time and that possession is identical and undivided. Failure to provide these prerequisites may be interpreted as creating a tenancy in common rather than a joint tenancy. In effect, joint tenants hold property as though they were one person.

TENANCY IN COMMON

As in joint tenancy ownership, each tenant is an owner with undivided interest in the whole property. Unlike joint tenancy, however, each tenant is personally liable for only his or her proportionate share of expenses incurred on the property. When one tenant dies, his or her share is passed on to their lawful heir or designee under the will. A tenant in common may also dispose of an ownership share by resale to another party, and the new owner takes his or her place as a tenant in common with the other owners.

The owners in common may each own equal shares, or the interests may differ in amount. Each owner's share in the income as well as in the expenses is proportionate to ownership. Owners may have acquired their interest at different times and under different conveyances. Moreover, tenants in common have the right to divide up the property according to ownership interest if such partition is feasible, or one of the owners may force the sale by filing appropriate legal action that would provide for liquidating the property and paying each owner their share of the proceeds.

GENERAL PARTNERSHIPS

Partnerships can be formed by two or more individuals who act as co-owners for profit. Unlike limited partnerships, each of the partners has a voice in the overall management and decision-making process. Ownership of the property is in the name of the partners individually, and each participates in execution of the conveyance instrument unless the partners empower a single partner to take the title in his or her name and act on behalf of the partnership.

In the event of death, the real property does not become a part of the deceased partner's estate, but reverts to the remaining partners. The partnership is obligated to reimburse the estate of the deceased, of course, by an amount equal to the value of his or her interest.

It is important to note that all of the assets of a joint partner are liable to partnership debts. Stated another way: Complete personal liability of each partner for all of the debts of the business and the acts of any partner acting within the scope of their authority in the partnership legally binds all other partners. This liability exposure is a major concern and probably the reason for the declining use of partnerships in property ownership.

As is true with the limited partnership, a general partnership is not taxed as a separate entity. An informational income tax return is filed, which describes the income or loss related to each partner's interest and which each partner carries into his or her own income tax return.

JOINT VENTURES

A joint venture is a special association formed for the purpose and intent of carrying out a special project or investment, with no intent of maintaining a continuing relationship. In other words, the parties are coventurers for a specific purpose.

From an income tax standpoint, the joint venture is treated much the same as the partnership. It is similar to a partnership in most other respects, as well. Most important, the members of a joint venture are personally liable for the debt and obligations of the venture in the same manner as general partners.

CORPORATIONS

A general corporation, also known as a C Corporation, formed to own real estate has several appealing features. These include perpetuity, liability limited to the ownership share of stock, and good liquidity of ownership through the transferability of stock. It may also be appealing to a group of investors who desire a continuing association in real estate ventures. From a negative standpoint, double taxation is one of the major concerns. The corporation pays federal taxes on its net income before distribution of dividends to shareholders. Income thus distributed to shareholders is taxed a second time under personal income tax laws. In addition to the payment of double taxes to the federal government, many states have corporate and personal income tax laws, further aggravating the double tax exposure.

The limited liability advantage also loses some of its significance in view of the fact that, in the case of small corporations with limited capital, the owners are usually required to cosign or personally guarantee notes for funds borrowed from lending institutions. This cosigning by all of the owners can be particularly inequitable since individuals with relatively small ownership shares in the corporation could conceivably be relatively strong from a personal financial standpoint. In the event that the bank had to exercise its loan guarantee provisions, it would be under no obligation to distinguish among the guarantors on the basis of ownership share in the corporation.

Nevertheless, the corporate approach to group ownership may make sense in some cases, and you will need a good tax attorney to advise you on specifics. High tax bracket investors may find the approach advantageous if corporate tax rates are lower than the personal income tax rates of the owners. Earnings may be plowed back into the corporation rather than distributed as dividends, and returned to the owners at a future date in some form that permits more favorable tax treatment. For example, earnings may be retained and reinvested in additional properties owned by the corporation. The investor could extract funds by selling all or part of the stocks owned, assuming that the per-share value would have appreciated in value to reflect the growth in the corporation's net worth. The gain thus realized would be subject to capital gains tax treatment, assuming that the hold period and other requirements for such treatment are met. Alternatively, the corporation might be liquidated and a similar result achieved. However, such a strategy must be carried out in a manner compatible with tax regulations pertaining to collapsible corporations, and this is why professional expertise is so important. Some personal income can also be extracted from the corporation without exposure to double taxation in the form of salaries paid to owner/managers, provided such salaries are reasonable and justifiable. Another possibility for high tax bracket investors may be tax exempt gifts. The earnings would be retained in the corporation and ownership shares would be passed on by the owner to his or her children in incremental annual amounts that fall within the allowable limits prescribed for tax exempt gifts by tax laws.

The double taxation problem with corporations can also be avoided through what is referred to as the S Corporation provision of the Internal Revenue Code, provided the small business corporations qualify and elect to function under this provision. S Corporations are not taxed in the same way as other corporations.

Instead, the tax treatment is similar to that for partnerships. Tax liability for corporate income is passed on to the stockholders, each of whom pays an individual tax on his or her allocated share, and such tax is paid regardless of whether the corporate income is distributed or retained. In order to qualify for this arrangement, the corporation must be domestic; have no more than a specified number of stockholders; derive not more than a specified share of its income from outside of the United States; have only one class of stock; derive not more than a specified share of its income from passive investments such as holding companies; and retain the continuity of life characteristics of a corporation. There are other provisions as well, and some of the important distinctions between conventional and S Corporations are summarized in Figure 11-1.

LIMITED LIABILITY COMPANIES (LLC)

The Limited Liability Company is neither a partnership nor a corporation, but contains selected elements that are common to both. For some businesses it may offer the best of all worlds. Like partnerships, LLCs are not subject to double taxation, as is true for C Corporations. With a properly formed LLC, all income passes through to the owners. Yet LLCs provide the protection from personal liability that a corporation affords. Ownership shares are more easily transferred than is true for a partnership, although less so than for a corporation. Owners of an LLC are called members, and members can sell their ownership interest to others, but it requires the consent of a majority of the other members. LLCs are managed by a manager, rather than by a president or general partner. An LLC also allows all members to participate in the management of the business without incurring personal liability, unlike the restrictions governing the limited partners of a limited partnership. An LLC must have at least two members, otherwise it is treated for tax purposes as a sole proprietorship. Unlike an S Corporation, there is no limitation on the number of owners or members and it is much easier to structure the distribution of earnings. In order for an LLC to qualify for such designation, it must possess no more than two of the four characteristics defined by the IRS Code as describing corporations. These are: limited liability, continuity of life, centralized (nonowner) management, and free transferability

FIGURE 11–1

Comparison of Selected Factors, Conventional (C) versus
S Corporations

	C Corporation	S Corporation
Origin of Operating Capital	Sale of common stocks, bonds, other securities, and loans.	Sale of one class of stock to no more than 75 shareholders.
Income Tax Treatment	Two-tier tax. First at corporate level on corporate earnings; second, at individual level on dividends distributed to shareholders.	Single tax applied to shareholders' portion of income, regardless of whether distributed.
Capital Gains Tax	Taxed at corporate level at corporate rates or at the alternative flat tax.	Taxed at shareholder level on net gain after deduction of operating loss.
Capital Losses	Deducted at corporate level but not in excess of capital gains. May be carried back or forward several years.	Not passed through to shareholders. Offset current capital gains; may be carried over against future capital gains.
Undistributed Earnings	May be accumulated for reasonable business needs, permitting deferral of dividend distribution and taxation at shareholder level. If the corporation does not distribute dividends, income earned by the corporation will be taxed to the shareholder as capital gain when shareholder sells shares.	All income, including accumulated, is passed through and taxed at shareholder level.
Net Operating Losses	No pass-through to shareholders.	Passed through to shareholders, but may not exceed shareholders' basis.
Liability Exposure	Generally liable for capital contributions only.	

of ownership. One key characteristic of the LLC that is the same as
for corporations is limited liability. With regard to the remaining
three characteristics, it is usually quite realistic for LLCs to avoid at
least two of them. Members are often actively engaged in the business's management of LLCs. Most LLCs can also be successfully
structured either without the continuity of life characteristic or
without free transferability of ownership. Clearly, some trade-offs
may have to be made in this regard, depending upon what is most

important for the specific venture or business for which the LLC is contemplated.

TRUSTS

Trusts represent entities that hold and administer property for the profit and advantage of a beneficiary. Real estate investment trusts, commonly referred to as REITs, came into being in the early 1960s with the enactment of legislation that exempted such trusts from the corporate net income tax on distributed earnings. To some degree, REITs became to real estate what mutual funds are to the stock market. They offer the opportunity to small investors to purchase a share of ownership in a diversified portfolio of real estate properties. However, unlike mutual funds, at least the open-end variety, REITs do not redeem shares. If the owner decides to liquidate, he or she must sell his or her shares to other investors. In this respect, they resemble limited partnerships, although the transfer of such ownership is much easier, particularly for large, well-established REITs handled by brokerage houses.

Figure 11-2 depicts the ownership and management concepts inherent in REITs and in some of the other major group investment types described in this chapter.

FIGURE 11–2

Ownership/Management Concepts—Group Investments

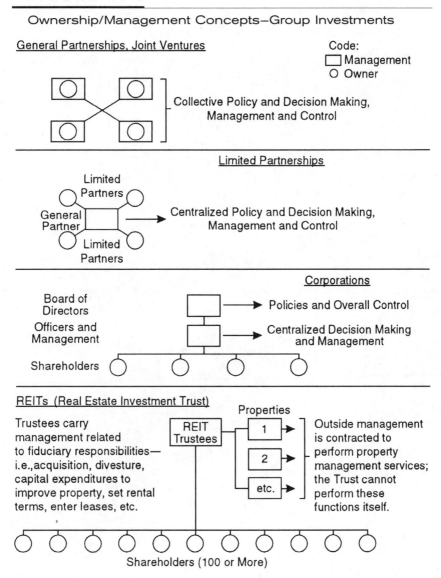

General Partnerships, Joint Ventures

Code:
☐ Management
○ Owner

Collective Policy and Decision Making,
Management and Control

Limited Partnerships

Limited Partners

General Partner

Limited Partners

Centralized Policy and Decision Making,
Management and Control

Corporations

Board of Directors

Officers and Management

Shareholders

Policies and Overall Control

Centralized Decision Making
and Management

REITs (Real Estate Investment Trust)

Properties

Trustees carry
management related
to fiduciary responsibilities—
i.e.,acquisition, divesture,
capital expenditures to
improve property, set rental
terms, enter leases, etc.

REIT Trustees

1
2
etc.

Outside management
is contracted to
perform property
management services;
the Trust cannot
perform these
functions itself.

Shareholders (100 or More)

CHAPTER 12

Using the Internet

The Internet is playing an ever-increasing role in our daily lives, and real estate is no exception. It has impacted the real estate industry by shifting more control to the individual, whether they be buyers or sellers, investors or consumers. An area of significant change is research. For example, a wide selection of websites now make it possible for home buyers to study a home's description, dimensions, and photographs before consulting a real estate agent. They can also use the Internet to determine mortgage rates, property tax rates, or find out about schools and local amenities for a specific neighborhood.

From an investor perspective, the accessibility of information concerning all types of real estate facilitates the process of searching, buying, financing, renting, or obtaining other important information. Even if investors themselves have not become proficient in using the Internet, they still benefit by the enhanced capabilities it provides to real estate agents who act on their behalf. While the Internet has already become a useful tool in real estate investment, its application and importance will continue to grow along with the use of personal computers. This chapter touches upon some of the highlights, but for those who intend to make wide use of the Internet in real estate applications, additional study will be required. There are a number of good books devoted to this subject, and if you are an Internet novice, consider starting with *The Complete Idiot's Guide to Online Buying and Selling a Home* by

Matthew O'Brien (published by Que, 2000). But since there are new books on the subject constantly coming out, it would be wise to also check with your local library or bookstore, or search the Net for the latest offerings. Regard the Internet as another useful tool for facilitating real estate investment goals, and one with which you should become sufficiently familiar to maximize achievement of these goals.

To access the Internet, of course, requires the use of one of the multitude of online service providers, such as America Online, Netscape, CompuServe, or the Microsoft Network, to name a few. Or you can do so through one of the multitude of small local providers. To search out a specific topic requires that you log on to one of the search engines available (directories or indexes like Alta Vista, Yahoo, Lycos, Excite) and type in the key words or phrases that you want searched. The other option is to go directly to one of the many websites that specialize in real estate information. Some of these sites are mentioned below. However, recognize that the Internet is an environment of rapid and continuous change. Accordingly, some of the Web addresses mentioned could change or disappear entirely, and new sites come into existence by the time you read this. In fact, such an outcome is virtually assured. So, use the information as illustrative of Internet applications, rather than as a complete, unchanging guide as to where to go on the Net. *The Real Estate Finance Journal* usually provides an updated listing of useful websites for real estate professionals in each of its issues. Or you might want to search the Net for the most current sites that specialize in real estate information.

A buyer, for example, can find listings of single family homes that are for sale. This would be useful for those interested in rental house investments. These lists are provided on a number of websites. Some of the major ones are HomeAdvisor (*homeadvisor.msn.com*), iOwn (*iown.com*), CyberHomes (*cyberhomes.com*), and Realtor.com (*realtor.com*). (Note that Internet addresses are always preceding by *www.* and are usually followed by *.com.* In the examples provided, we have dropped the ubiquitous *www.* prefix. There are many other relevant websites. Real Select operates Realtor.com for the National Association of Realtors and is reported to have 1.3 million home listings at the time of this writing. Microsoft's HomeAdvisor has about 400,000 listings, is considered by many to be among the easiest to use, and shoppers can view listings according to five key areas: how much can I afford, finding a neighborhood, finding a home, finding a loan, and offer and closing. Each site has certain advantages and disadvantages, and the investor who intends to use one or more needs to explore each to determine which best meets his or her particular needs. They all have much to offer. Additional websites you may want to explore in this regard are: *amshomefinder.com, bagi.com, century21.com, homeseekers.com,* and *relocate-america.com.*

However, for the investor using a real estate agent or broker to locate properties, it may make more sense not to become unduly embroiled in such searches, which can become time consuming and complex. Instead, you may choose to leave such searches to the real estate professionals who are probably more adept at it and are being paid a commission to provide such service. Moreover, if the homes you are searching on the Internet are listed with a real estate broker, the seller will pay the real estate commission and you will not realize any savings by not using a real estate agent.

For do-it-yourself investors who seek to deal with the sellers apart from real estate agents, there are *For Sale by Owner* websites, which are precisely what the name implies. They are home sites not listed with real estate firms. Two such sites are Owners.com (*owners.com*) and FSBO.COM (*fsbo.com*). The obvious catch to saving money by purchasing directly from the seller is that both the seller and buyer are seeking to reap a financial benefit by eliminating the use of a real estate middleman. Nevertheless, the potential exists for negotiating a better price under this approach.

From the seller's perspective, these websites represent a marketing tool. In the case of "For Sale by Owner" sites, there may be a charge to the seller. Although there is usually no charge for a simple written description, a modest fee is charged for listings that include a photograph, or possibly several photographs and a layout of the property. The charge increases with the amount of pictorial exposure. But the amount paid is well worth the cost, and covers listing the property for several months. The significance of the Internet as either a purchase or sales tool is evidenced by the growing number of people using it these days. Matthew O'Brien, in his book, reports that about 20 percent of all buyers and sellers are using the Internet for this purpose in the year 2000, up from 5 percent two years earlier. Such use is expected to continue to rise.

If you are searching for vacant lots or land, one approach is to log on to the Board of Realtors for your area. Their Web address can be obtained through the National Association of Realtors (*realtor.com*). After going to the local Board of Realtors site, follow through by sequentially going to property search, type of property (i.e., residential or commercial, vacant lots, farm or agricultural land), county involved, and other information pertinent to your search (i.e., price range, acreage, etc.).

Selecting a lending institution is another real estate application offered by the Internet. Among the online lending sites are Quicken Mortgage (*quickenmortgage.com*), E-LOAN (*eloan.com*), and Lending Tree.com (*lendingtree.com*). You can also go to any of the home buyer sites mentioned earlier, such as HomeAdvisor, CyberHomes, iOwn, REALTOR.COM, or any of the many other megasites that offer a complete spectrum of search services, including homesites, information on neighborhoods, and demographic data. Or, if you want to check out a specific lender, you can go directly to their Web addresses by logging in their name, preceded by *www.* and followed by *.com.* You can visit these different sites to determine interest rates offered, fees, closing costs, points charged, loan repayment penalties, and other information that may be important in a loan decision.

Locating a real estate agent is still another application of the Internet. The National Association of Realtors (NAR) is a good source for this (*realtor.com*). Or, information is accessible on the offices and agents of specific real estate franchises or chains in your area by entering its name, again preceded by *www.* and followed by *.com.* The selection of a real estate agent obviously involves much more than getting a name and location from the Internet. It requires an interview to determine experience, track record, areas of expertise by types of property, references, as well as determination of overall compatibility in terms of personalities and the level of confidence you feel you can place in the individual. Nevertheless, if you are not already working with a specific agent, the Net may be a good place to start, especially if you are seeking a particular type of real estate professional.

Determining the value of property you own is an important prerequisite to selling it. Realtors do this through what is called a comparative market analysis. A CMA consists of determining what real estate properties comparable to the one you are selling in that particular locality have sold for during the past year or two. Real estate agents are very good at this and normally provide CMAs as a service for clients whose property they have been retained to sell. Agents have access to the Multiple Listing Service (MLS) system, which is a very detailed and comprehensive source for sale price data, particularly concerning homes. They are also generally familiar with the area of the property being sold and the value of such properties. However, there are websites that do-it-yourself investors can use to get comparative market prices. These include DataQuick (*dataquick.com*), HomeGain.com (*homegain.com*), and Experian (*experian.com*). There is a charge for each property for which comparable sales information is obtained. These services are used mostly for homes. Determining the value of apartment complexes, which is largely determined by the income it produces, is more aptly done using a financial analysis technique explained elsewhere. In the case of land, available sites are typically much more widespread geographically than homes, and their features or characteristics vary so widely that CMAs are usually best accomplished under a more customized approach that reflects the experience of real estate agents or investors familiar with land values in the area.

Although there is a wide range and growing body of information pertaining to real estate available on the Internet, many investors are not inclined to devote the time necessary to become highly proficient in its use, which can become time consuming. Moreover, much real estate on the Internet is oriented toward consumers rather than investors. By consumers, I am referring to home buyers and renters. Real estate agents, on the other hand, have access to much more investor-oriented information through the Multiple Listing Service to which they subscribe, as well as other information services available to brokers, often at a substantial cost. For those involved in real estate investment as an avocation rather than a vocation, it is usually more cost and time effective to utilize the services of real estate agents in locating investment opportunities, whether this involves rental houses, apartment buildings, or land. The information benefits of the Internet will still be realized but will be achieved through those who are much more adept and better equipped to conduct such searches. And, as already mentioned, since the seller pays the real estate commission, it makes little sense to avoid the use of competent real estate agents on the buy end of real estate transactions.

With regard to the selling or renting aspects of real estate investment, on the other hand, the use of the Internet by the investor makes more sense. In such functions it can be a tool for marketing directly to the consumer (renter or buyer) apart from real estate agents, providing the potential for savings in commissions or rental fees. However, even this is questionable. Real estate agents have much better access to the market for both potential buyers and renters. Moreover, the real opportunity for profitable real estate investing lies primarily in the selection of properties that will appreciate rapidly in value and, in the case of rental properties, maintain high occupancy rates. Achieving these goals is usually enhanced through the services of good real estate agents, and the benefits of such services usually outweigh any financial cost savings achievable through reduced real estate commissions or similar costs by using the Internet. Much depends upon the investor's personal situation in terms of available time to devote to investment activity and proficiency in using the Internet, as well as such factors as the nature of the investment property involved, prevailing market conditions, and the constantly improving nature of information and services available through the Internet.

CHAPTER 13

Real Estate Brokers

Most investors rely on real estate brokers to buy and sell properties. Brokers can be a valuable asset to investors. Going it alone is possible but usually not wise or cost effective. The primary motivation to invest without using a broker is the potential to save on commissions. But unless you have an active real estate license yourself, the potential for such savings may prove to be illusionary more often than not. Most properties on the market and available to you as an investor will be listed with real estate brokers. Excluding such listings narrows the field of potential prospects considerably. Assuming that you do end up buying property that is listed with a real estate broker, the cost of such commission is usually reflected in the price. Therefore, you will probably not achieve a price benefit, even if you locate the property on your own. If you are a licensed broker, you might be able to split the commission with the listing brokerage firm, and thus achieve a financial benefit. Otherwise, a financial benefit is questionable unless the listing broker is willing to reduce his or her commission, which is unlikely.

If you are selling property apart from a broker, you will avoid a real estate commission provided you are able to market the property successfully. The prospects for achieving a financial benefit through a do-it-yourself approach are much better on the selling end of the real estate transaction than on the buying end. This is true because of opportunities by way of the Internet, as discussed in Chapter 12.

However, it is unlikely that the average investor can market proper- ties as effectively as a broker. Professionals have access to the Multiple Listing Service (MLS), as well as a wide range of Internet services which they are very proficient at using. Moreover, selling is an art, and the limited number of potential buyers who feel comfort- able in buying apart from a broker narrows the field of prospective buyers considerably. Most buyers are much more comfortable having a broker conduct the search, inspection, evaluation, negotiations, financing, and other purchase functions on their behalf.

In selecting a broker it is important to recognize that all are not alike. Although all brokers are legally able to sell all types of property, some specialize in commercial properties, others in apart- ment buildings, others in single family houses, and still others in land. It is important to select one who specializes in the type of property you are buying or selling. Brokers who specialize in com- mercial properties are usually equipped to perform cash flow and internal rate of return analyses through specialized computer pro- grams. Most large real estate franchises have divisions that spe- cialize in various types of properties, and the manager or broker in most branch offices can provide referrals. The commission struc- ture for commercial or industrial properties may vary depending on the value of the property involved.

The terms *agent, realtor,* and *broker* are often used interchange- ably, but it is important to recognize the distinctions among them. Brokers are licensed to buy, sell, exchange, or lease property for others in exchange for a fee. Agents or real estate salespersons are licensed to sell real estate as representatives of the broker for whom they work. Brokers can own or manage a real estate office; agents cannot. Realtors are agents or brokers who are affiliated with the National Association of Realtors, which has organizations at both the state and national levels. Realtors agree to conform to the code of ethics of the association, agree to pay annual dues to maintain membership and, in the event of disputes arising under a transac- tion, must abide by its decision in dispute resolution.

SELLERS VERSUS BUYERS AGENTS

There are sellers' brokerages or agents and buyers' brokerages or agents. As the names imply, sellers' brokerages work for the sellers, and buyers' brokerages work for the buyers. There are also dual agency brokerages that can represent either buyers or sellers, but usually not on the same transaction. Buyers should use buyers' brokers for a number of reasons, the most obvious being that these brokers or agents work with the buyers' best interests in mind. Most good buyers' brokers do not list properties, which means they focus upon locating the best properties and price for their clients, rather than upon obtaining listings. Moreover, it usually does not cost the buyer anything. Most sellers' brokers split commissions with buyers' brokers, which means that sellers pay the real estate commission. Buyers' brokers can be paid by the buyers, but this is usually the exception. In such cases the buyer may sign an exclusive buyer contract agreeing to pay the agent a fee, and the agent, in turn, agrees not to accept a commission from the seller or the seller's real estate agent. This establishes a fiduciary responsibility in which the buyer's broker is obligated to act in the best interests of the buyer and to use his or her abilities and resources to get the property at the best price and terms.

In an earlier era, almost all brokers were sellers' brokers. Even today, many buyers continue to use them. In such cases it is important to remember that the broker represents the seller, even though he works with you as a buyer. Although sellers' brokers are legally obligated to be honest and fair with buyers, their loyalty and fiduciary responsibility is with the seller. Accordingly, what is intended as confidential information by the buyer may be passed on to the seller by the broker if he or she is made privy to such information. For example, if the buyer wants to make an offer below the asking price on property presented by the seller's agent but indicates to the agent a willingness to increase the amount offered if rejected by the seller, such information will be passed on by the agent to the seller. So, if you use a seller's agent in purchasing property, keep your game plan to yourself.

DUAL AGENCY

Normally, a broker represents only one party in a transaction. This is called *single agency.* The party represented can be either the buyer or the seller. The broker can represent both buyers and sellers, but not for the same transaction. This assures loyalty to the client represented and avoids conflict of interest. In the case of *dual agency*, the brokerage firm represents both the buyer and seller in the same transaction. For example, a single agent of the brokerage firm might represent both the buyer and seller for a given transaction. Or it could involve two agents from the same firm, whereby one agent represents the seller and the other the buyer. Because both agents work for the same broker in this transaction, the agency relationship becomes dual, even though each agent represents a different party.

The potential exists under such an arrangement for an exchange of information between the two agents that may be intended to be confidential on the part of either the buyer or seller or both. The challenge of fulfilling the fiduciary obligations to both parties without compromising either, particularly if the parties' interests are conflicting, is therefore a difficult one. Many contend that it is questionable whether a dual agent can ever fully represent either party's interests in an optimal manner. The risks range from abuse of trust to conflicts of interest. For this reason it is illegal in some states, and where it is legal, all parties must consent to it.

Those who defend dual agency point out certain advantages and safeguards. Statutory requirements assure that buyers and sellers are made aware of the relationship and the fiduciary responsibility of the brokerage firm to those with whom they are working. Since the brokerage firm has a larger commission to work with under this arrangement, it can draw from such funds to solve last minute disputes that may arise between buyer and seller. For example, the broker may be willing to pay for certain incidentals whose responsibility the parties cannot agree upon. Information can also flow more quickly where the two agents know each other and work cooperatively.

CHAPTER 14

A Word about Financing

Mortgages, trust deeds, and contracts of sale are three commonly used legal instruments to finance real estate transactions, and about which there may be some confusion. Mortgages and trust deeds (or deeds of trust) are similar in many respects. In the use of either, there are two documents involved: a promissory note to pay, and a mortgage or trust deed that makes collateral of the property to secure the loan. In the case of a mortgage, two parties are involved: the borrower (mortgagor) and the lender (mortgagee). The mortgage does not convey title but in effect gives the lender a lien on the property as security for the loan. A trust deed involves three parties: the borrower (trustor), the lender (beneficiary), and the trustee (usually a title company or bank). The title to the property is conveyed to the trustee by the borrower as security for debt to the lender. When the borrower has fulfilled the terms of the loan and paid back the amount owed to the lender, the title is reconveyed to the borrower. If the borrower defaults on the loan, the trustee disposes of or liquidates the property at public sale in order to satisfy the debt. The use of mortgages and trust deeds varies by state. Most states permit the use of one or the other. A few states permit the use of both.

The terms *mortgage* and *trust deed* are used interchangeably in the ensuing discussion. The trust deed is usually preferred by investors because it permits easier foreclosure. Mortgages generally tend to provide greater protection to the borrower through redemption opportunities and the requirement for more time-consuming foreclosure proceedings. Laws in this regard differ by state.

Variable rate mortgages are a more recent innovation in conventional loans. These loans have fluctuating interest rates designed to rise and fall with the money markets. The adjustment of the interest rate is accomplished at periodic reviews of prevailing rates, usually several times a year. In periods of rising interest rates, variable rates are a disadvantage to the investor. A positive feature is that such loans are usually fully assumable, provided the new buyer's credit is approved.

The *contract of sale* (also called *land contract, installment contract,* and a variety of other names usually involving the word *contract*) provides another loan approach that can be quite useful. This is a loan directly from the seller, who retains title to the property until the terms of the loan are fulfilled. A key advantage is flexibility. The buyer and seller can structure the terms to meet their own unique requirements and objectives, and there are no loan fees involved. This instrument is often used in transactions involving very low down payments or during tight money periods when financing from lending institutions is difficult to obtain. It is also common in transactions involving raw land since conventional lending institutions normally will not finance such property. Although it can be a useful legal instrument, it should be drawn up by a competent attorney to protect both parties. Since the buyer does not take title to the property until the debt is fully paid and the terms of the agreement are fulfilled, legal action may be required to acquire title in the event the lender dies or becomes incompetent. It is therefore important that the contract be recorded and that title insurance be issued to both seller and buyer. The contract should also include provision for remedy in the event of default by either buyer or seller.

Second-position mortgages or trust deeds represent another alternative, for which both institutional and noninstitutional lenders are potential sources. These are legal instruments to borrow money from someone, with a loan that is secured by the property owned by the borrower. However, the property owned by the borrower and used to secure the loan already has a first mortgage. The loan is therefore subordinated to this first mortgage. To illustrate, assume that the buyer owns a house worth $100,000 in which the equity is $40,000. Even though there is a first mortgage to secure the $60,000 balance, many lenders would be willing to provide a loan secured by the same property under a second mortgage because of the owner's equity. It is usually possible to borrow about 75 percent of the value of such equity, or in this case about $30,000. Although the second is subordinated to the first mortgage, the lender is quite well protected.

SOME SECOND MORTGAGE STRATEGIES

Second-position mortgages represent an effective technique for minimizing the investor's equity investment. This is particularly true for desirable assumptions in which the seller's equity has increased beyond the level of a normal down payment. Several variations are possible:

1. The most desirable approach is to give the seller a note secured by a second mortgage for the amount of money owed. To illustrate, consider the purchase of a $300,000 apartment building under an arrangement in which the buyer is to assume the existing loan, which has a balance of $200,000. The buyer owes the seller $100,000 for equity. Rather than paying cash, the buyer might offer the seller a $30,000 down payment plus a note for the remaining $70,000, secured by a second mortgage. Since banks will normally refuse a new loan under an arrangement in which the buyer finances the down payment, this approach works best where the buyer assumes an existing loan. Unfortunately, assumable loans under favorable terms are frequently not available.

2. A variation is to give the seller a second mortgage on other real estate owned by the buyer. In effect, the seller advances the buyer the money required for the down payment, which is then returned. This circumvents the objections by banks described in the preceding paragraph with respect to new loans.

3. A third possibility is to raise the funds needed for the down payment from a third party, rather than from the seller. This approach may be appropriate if the seller needs cash for equity and refuses to participate in second mortgage financing under either of the preceding approaches. Private parties are usually preferable to institutions as financing sources under this approach. Bankers and real estate attorneys are possible sources for recommending private parties interested in this type of investment. Less desirable third-party sources are real estate brokers or mortgage investment

brokers. They are less desirable because of loan fees or commissions charged to locate lenders. Other less desirable sources are the so-called hard money lenders: commercial banks, thrift institutions, finance companies, credit unions, and so on. Not only are terms generally less favorable, but additional costs such as loan fees and appraisal costs are involved.

4. Another second mortgage approach is the wraparound mortgage, also referred to as the all-inclusive or overriding mortgage. In this approach, the buyer gives a mortgage for the entire amount of indebtedness. This mortgage is subordinate to but includes the indebtedness of the first mortgage plus the seller's equity. To illustrate, consider again the preceding example involving a $300,000 apartment building having an existing mortgage with a balance of $200,000. The buyer is willing to pay $30,000 down and finance the balance. Under the wraparound approach, the buyer gives the seller a note for the total balance of $270,000, which would include the unpaid balance of the first mortgage. In most cases, the buyer pays the seller the full mortgage payment, and the seller continues to make the payments on the first mortgage. The wraparound mortgage is at an interest rate higher than that of the first mortgage. In the case of a simple second mortgage on seller's equity, the total interest income is a percentage of the amount of such equity. Here, though, the seller receives an additional income in interest payments since the wraparound mortgage is written at a higher interest rate than that of the first mortgage. The seller not only receives a full interest payment on his or her equity, but gains on the balance of the first mortgage loan by the differential between these two interest rates. Advantages to the buyer are more favorable terms, lower down payment, and reduced financing costs.

Although lending institutions would require a higher down payment on a new loan for the purchase described and would not advance funds on a second mortgage, they are well covered under the wraparound approach. This is because the seller continues to make the same payments to the lending institution, and the wraparound mortgage is subordinate to the first mortgage. In the event of default, the first mortgage holder still has prior claim. This approach is limited to cases where the first loan has no acceleration clause or provisions that preclude its use. It is obviously less appealing to the investor than a simple second mortgage or trust deed on the seller's equity, but it may be a good alternative if the seller rejects such an approach.

These second mortgage strategies not only reduce the investor's cash requirement but also transfer part of the risk from the buyer to the second mortgage holder. To illustrate, consider the implications of an unexpected drop in the value of an investment property to less than the original price paid by the investor. In the event that the investor concurrently experiences unanticipated financial difficulties (such as job loss) and is unable to meet mortgage payment obligations, the property would be repossessed to meet creditor demands. The holder of the first mortgage would probably recover his or her money without difficulty since the original loan amount was substantially lower than the purchase price. However, the holder of the second mortgage might recover only a portion of the amount he or she loaned due to the drop in value and the fact that their claim is subordinated to the first mortgage. The borrower is still personally responsible for this loan, and the lender could conceivably recover the amount owed through other assets belonging to the borrower. However, as a practical matter, if the borrower is in financial difficulty it may be costly, time consuming, or impossible to recover the balance owed. The second mortgage holder could therefore incur the loss that would otherwise be borne by the investor.

ASSUMING AN EXISTING MORTGAGE

Assumptions involve taking over an existing mortgage. This used to be a viable option but opportunities are more limited today since most mortgages now require that the balance owed on the mortgage be paid upon sale of the property. Although most loans are theoretically assumable subject to lending institution approval, the process of obtaining such approval is much the same as getting approval for a new loan.

FHA PROGRAMS

If you are purchasing property that needs substantial repair, or renovation, the Federal Housing Administration (FHA) may have a program of interest. The FHA 203(k) is an insurance program designed to make it possible for buyers to get loans to fix up rundown properties in deteriorating or disadvantaged neighborhoods, where affordable conventional loans would be difficult to find. Under this program, investors as well as home owners can get loans that cover both the price of the property and the cost of repairs or renovation. The government's intent is to stimulate the improvement of homes and buildings in run-down neighborhoods by facilitating access to favorable loan terms (low down payments and low interest rates). There are certain mortgage limits that apply, and since the rules are subject to periodic change, the local Department of Housing and Urban Development (HUD) office should be contacted for the latest specifics. The program is generally oriented toward one- to-four-family residential housing.

You may also find the HUD Title I home improvement loan program worth investigating. This program makes it easier to obtain home improvement loans by insuring the loans that qualify. There are limits on the loan amounts available under this program for improving either single family homes or multifamily structures. Again, these limits are subject to change and HUD should be contacted to get the current specifics. To obtain such information on either the FHA 203(k) program or the HUD Title I program, HUD is listed under U.S. Government offices in your telephone directory. Call for forms and directives or for an information packet.

OTHER POSSIBILITIES

The financing package must be structured to accommodate the specific needs of the parties involved and the unique circumstances of each investment. Once an attractive investment property is located, alternative financing arrangements and strategies should be conceived and then tested through the negotiating process. For example, assume that the money market is extremely tight and financing from conventional lending institutions for the purchase of investment properties involves unacceptable terms (high down payment, high interest rates, and high loan fees). If none of the suggested mortgage approaches work, either because of seller reluctance or other reasons, a contract directly with the seller is always a possibility. Although this may not seem promising in view of the fact that the seller rejected the second mortgage approach, it could be that the rejection was based upon a reluctance concerning second mortgages rather than a need for cash. A direct contract proposal might therefore represent a strategy worth exploring and should be structured around a low down payment, long contract period, and low interest rate. If the seller needs substantial cash and is reluctant to sell on a contract basis unless a large down payment is received, the buyer might consider refinancing or taking out a second mortgage on his or her own home if a large equity exists. This approach usually permits conventional financing under more favorable terms, even in a tight money market, since the property involved is an owner-occupied dwelling. The undesirable aspect of this variation is that it utilizes the buyer's existing equity assets rather than the investment property to secure the loan. However, if the buyer plans no alternate use of these assets, it might be a desirable approach, particularly if the accompanying terms are attractive. The large down payment could be liquidated at a later date by refinancing the property when interest rates drop and the money market softens.

Another possibility, depending upon the personal motivation, interests, and circumstances of the buyer, is to represent the property as an owner-occupied dwelling and obtain conventional financing. (Keep in mind the assumption that conventional financing is available only for owner-occupied dwellings—not for investment properties—due to the tight money market hypothesized.) In this case the buyer would move into the house for a period of six months or so and lease his or her current home. This alternative is particularly suitable when the property needs repairs or renovation and the buyer is interested in this approach to value building.

The intent of the preceding discussion has been to emphasize that financing must be tailored to the environment as well as to the investor's circumstances. Instead of locating a desirable property and then formulating financing strategy, it may at times be desirable to reverse this sequence. That is, it may be better to first define the type of financing approach desired and then limit the search for properties that conform to this constraint. This is particularly true during periods of abnormal money markets.

EXCHANGES

The subject of tax-free exchanges is related closely enough to financing to warrant brief comment. The sale of investment property for cash requires the payment of income taxes on the gain. Contrary to popular misconception, reinvesting the proceeds in another more valuable investment property within a given time period does not defer the tax obligation. One way of accomplishing such deferral is to exchange the property for another of higher value. If it is exchanged for property of lower value, or if the exchange is for anything other than real estate, there will probably be a tax obligation. Tax regulations pertaining to exchanges are complicated, and it is critically important that the investor enlist the services of a good tax attorney or accountant experienced in property exchanges.

Exchanges are often used with respect to apartment building investments and other properties of substantial value where the tax exposure is significant. They can be quite complex, involving one-, two-, or three-way exchanges. There are realtors who specialize in this type of transaction, and it is advisable to use the services of such professionals if you decide to pursue this approach.

One type of exchange, if properly executed, permits the proceeds from the sale of a property to be used to buy another property and defer taxes. A provision in the Federal Tax Code, Section 1031, allows unlimited capital gains to be deferred indefinitely if the seller buys property of "like kind" within 180 days. This is a delayed exchange, sometimes referred to as "Starker type exchanges." It is named after T. J. Starker, an Oregon man, who made a deal in 1967 to exchange some of his property with Crown Zellerbach for some suitable future property. The agreement ended up in court and was the basis for congressional approval of delayed exchanges. The 1984 Tax Reform Act provided further clarification on the issue of such exchanges, as well as regulations subsequently issued by the IRS. "Like kind" at this writing is any property used for investment, income, or business purposes. The properties cannot be principal residences; the new property must be identified within 45 days following the sale of the property sold and transferred within 180 days after the first property is sold; and proceeds from the sale must be inaccessible to the investor or trader. The cost of the property purchased must equal or exceed the price of that sold, and the new mortgage must be as large or larger than that which existed on the property sold. There are other IRS rules, as well. As already emphasized, an attorney is an absolute necessity since the transactions require detailed documentation and a proper sequence of execution. Moreover, tax rules are frequently revised, making the services of an attorney or CPA essential. For example, revision of the definition of "like kind" has been under consideration from time to time and is subject to change of a more restrictive nature, should the rule makers so decide. Therefore, keep the basic concept in mind but be sure to check out the latest governing regulations before attempting to execute such a transaction. For further information the reader is advised to study Section 1031 of the Internal Revenue Code.

OPTIONS

The use of options represents another technique that is closely related to financing and that provides for substantial leverage of funds. Simply stated, an option is the payment of an amount to the seller in exchange for the right to buy the seller's property within a defined time period and at a certain price. Options have already been discussed as a strategy for tying up property while applying for a zone change to upgrade the property value. Options are also an effective instrument for putting a hold on undervalued property until it can be sold to a buyer at an increased price. To illustrate, suppose a buyer locates property for sale at $50,000, which is recognized to be substantially below its market value within the near future. Assume the true value to be about $55,000. Because of other commitments, the buyer is not currently postured to purchase the property and therefore decides to offer the seller $1000 in return for an option to buy within two years for $50,000. The rationale is that the property is already underpriced and is likely to further appreciate in value during the period of the option. If it is held for one year, during which it appreciates by 15 percent, it will be worth about $62,500. Even if selling costs of $5000 are incurred (real estate commission, closing costs, etc.), the investor earns a profit of $2500 on the $1000 option investment—a 250 percent return. In addition to an outstanding rate of return, the investor does not manage the property during the hold period and pays no taxes. It is evident that such a strategy offers real opportunities for astute investors who are on the alert for undervalued real estate. Some investors specialize in this approach. On the negative side, the option payment can be lost if the property cannot be resold at the expected increase in value.

Financing is a broad subject, and we have only touched upon a few ideas. Remember that borrowed money is simply a commodity that you buy with interest. Do not be intimidated by lending institutions that sometimes convey the impression that you are fortunate to receive their services. You are a customer, and you should expect to be treated as such. Shop around to find the best buy and the best service. It can vary substantially. Remember, too, that terms are frequently negotiable. The financing approach must be adapted to the times and circumstances. The type of arrangements emphasized during periods of tight money will necessarily differ from those used when money is plentiful. The key is to structure creative and innovative approaches to the circumstances of each investment opportunity.

APPENDIX A. MORTGAGE, CONTRACT, OR LOAN BALANCE TABLES

APPENDIX B. MORTGAGE, CONTRACT, OR LOAN PAYMENT TABLES

APPENDIX C. THE EFFECT OF DIFFERENT CAPITAL GAINS TAX RATE ASSUMPTIONS ON PROFITABILITY ANALYSIS CHARTS DATA OF CHAPTERS 5 AND 7

A. MORTGAGE, CONTRACT, OR LOAN BALANCE TABLES

These tables may be used to determine the balance owed on a loan, mortgage, or contract at any point in time. In order to use the tables, select the correct factor based on the original length of the loan in years, the current age in years, and the applicable interest rate. Multiply the original loan amount by this factor in order to determine the balance owed. Data is predicated upon the assumption of uniform monthly payments.

APPENDIX A-1

Mortgage, Contract, or Loan Balance Table

ORIGINAL PERIOD (YEARS)	AGE (YEARS)	BALANCE OWED AS A RATIO OF ORIGINAL AMOUNT FOR VARIOUS INTEREST RATES										
		5%	5¼%	6%	6½%	7%	7½%	8%	8½%	9%	9½%	10%
5	1	.819	.821	.823	.825	.827	.829	.831	.832	.834	.836	.838
	2	.629	.632	.635	.638	.641	.644	.647	.650	.653	.655	.658
	3	.430	.433	.436	.439	.442	.445	.448	.451	.454	.457	.460
	4	.220	.222	.224	.227	.228	.231	.233	.235	.237	.239	.242
10	1	.921	.923	.925	.927	.928	.930	.932	.934	.935	.937	.939
	2	.838	.841	.845	.848	.851	.855	.858	.861	.865	.868	.871
	3	.750	.755	.760	.764	.769	.773	.778	.783	.787	.792	.796
	4	.658	.664	.669	.675	.681	.686	.692	.697	.703	.708	.713
	5	.562	.568	.574	.580	.586	.592	.598	.604	.610	.616	.622
	6	.460	.466	.472	.479	.484	.490	.496	.503	.509	.515	.521
	7	.354	.359	.364	.370	.375	.381	.386	.393	.398	.404	.409
	8	.241	.245	.250	.255	.258	.263	.267	.273	.277	.282	.286
	9	.123	.125	.128	.132	.133	.135	.138	.142	.144	.148	.150
11	1	.930	.932	.934	.936	.937	.939	.941	.943	.944	.946	.947
	2	.856	.860	.864	.867	.870	.874	.877	.880	.883	.886	.889
	3	.779	.784	.789	.794	.798	.803	.807	.812	.816	.821	.825
	4	.698	.703	.710	.715	.721	.727	.732	.738	.743	.749	.754
	5	.612	.619	.625	.632	.638	.645	.651	.657	.663	.670	.676
	6	.522	.529	.536	.543	.549	.556	.563	.569	.575	.583	.589
	7	.428	.434	.441	.448	.454	.461	.467	.474	.480	.487	.494
	8	.328	.334	.340	.347	.352	.358	.364	.370	.375	.382	.388
	9	.224	.228	.234	.238	.242	.247	.252	.257	.260	.266	.271
	10	.114	.117	.120	.123	.125	.128	.130	.133	.135	.139	.142
12	1	.938	.939	.941	.943	.945	.946	.948	.950	.951	.953	.954
	2	.872	.875	.879	.882	.886	.889	.892	.895	.898	.901	.904
	3	.803	.808	.813	.818	.822	.827	.831	.836	.840	.844	.848
	4	.731	.736	.742	.748	.754	.760	.765	.771	.776	.782	.787
	5	.654	.661	.668	.675	.681	.687	.694	.700	.707	.713	.719
	6	.574	.581	.589	.596	.603	.610	.617	.624	.630	.638	.644
	7	.490	.497	.505	.512	.519	.526	.533	.540	.547	.555	.561
	8	.402	.408	.415	.422	.429	.435	.443	.449	.456	.463	.470
	9	.308	.314	.321	.327	.332	.338	.345	.350	.356	.363	.369
	10	.211	.214	.220	.225	.229	.233	.238	.243	.247	.253	.257
	11	.108	.109	.113	.116	.118	.120	.123	.125	.128	.132	.134

APPENDIX A-2

Mortgage, Contract, or Loan Balance Table

ORIGINAL PERIOD (YEARS)	AGE (YEARS)	BALANCE OWED AS A RATIO OF ORIGINAL AMOUNT FOR VARIOUS INTEREST RATES										
		5%	5½%	6%	6½%	7%	7½%	8%	8½%	9%	9½%	10%
13	1	.944	.946	.948	.949	.951	.953	.954	.956	.957	.959	.960
	2	.885	.888	.892	.895	.898	.902	.905	.908	.911	.914	.917
	3	.823	.828	.833	.837	.842	.847	.851	.856	.860	.864	.869
	4	.758	.764	.770	.776	.782	.787	.793	.799	.804	.810	.815
	5	.689	.696	.703	.710	.717	.724	.730	.737	.744	.750	.756
	6	.617	.625	.633	.640	.647	.655	.662	.669	.677	.684	.691
	7	.541	.550	.558	.565	.573	.581	.588	.596	.604	.612	.619
	8	.462	.470	.478	.485	.493	.501	.508	.516	.524	.532	.540
	9	.378	.386	.393	.400	.407	.415	.422	.429	.437	.445	.452
	10	.290	.297	.303	.309	.315	.322	.328	.335	.342	.348	.355
	11	.197	.203	.208	.212	.217	.222	.226	.232	.238	.243	.248
	12	.100	.104	.107	.109	.111	.114	.117	.120	.124	.127	.130
14	1	.949	.951	.953	.955	.956	.958	.960	.961	.963	.964	.965
	2	.896	.900	.903	.906	.909	.913	.916	.919	.922	.924	.927
	3	.840	.845	.850	.854	.859	.864	.868	.873	.877	.881	.885
	4	.781	.788	.793	.799	.805	.811	.817	.823	.828	.833	.838
	5	.720	.727	.733	.740	.748	.754	.761	.768	.775	.780	.786
	6	.655	.663	.670	.678	.686	.693	.701	.709	.716	.723	.729
	7	.586	.595	.602	.611	.619	.627	.635	.644	.652	.659	.667
	8	.515	.523	.531	.539	.548	.556	.564	.574	.582	.589	.597
	9	.439	.447	.455	.463	.471	.479	.488	.497	.505	.512	.520
	10	.360	.367	.374	.381	.390	.397	.405	.414	.421	.428	.435
	11	.276	.283	.288	.295	.302	.308	.315	.323	.330	.335	.341
	12	.189	.193	.197	.202	.208	.212	.217	.224	.229	.233	.237
	13	.097	.099	.100	.103	.107	.109	.112	.117	.120	.121	.123
15	1	.954	.956	.958	.959	.961	.962	.964	.965	.967	.968	.970
	2	.906	.909	.913	.916	.919	.922	.925	.928	.931	.933	.936
	3	.855	.860	.865	.869	.874	.878	.883	.887	.891	.894	.899
	4	.802	.807	.814	.819	.826	.831	.837	.842	.848	.853	.858
	5	.745	.752	.760	.767	.774	.780	.787	.794	.800	.806	.813
	6	.686	.694	.703	.710	.719	.725	.734	.741	.748	.755	.763
	7	.624	.632	.642	.650	.659	.667	.676	.684	.691	.699	.708
	8	.559	.567	.577	.586	.595	.603	.613	.621	.629	.638	.647
	9	.491	.499	.509	.517	.527	.535	.545	.553	.561	.570	.579
	10	.419	.426	.436	.444	.454	.461	.471	.479	.487	.496	.505

APPENDIX A-3

Mortgage, Contract, or Loan Balance Table

ORIGINAL PERIOD (YEARS)	AGE (YEARS)	BALANCE OWED AS A RATIO OF ORIGINAL AMOUNT FOR VARIOUS INTEREST RATES										
		5%	5½%	6%	6½%	7%	7½%	8%	8½%	9%	9½%	10%
15	11	.343	.350	.359	.366	.375	.381	.391	.399	.406	.414	.423
	12	.264	.269	.277	.282	.291	.296	.304	.311	.317	.324	.332
	13	.180	.183	.190	.193	.200	.203	.210	.216	.220	.225	.232
	14	.092	.093	.098	.099	.103	.104	.109	.112	.114	.116	.121
16	1	.958	.960	.962	.963	.965	.966	.968	.969	.971	.972	.973
	2	.914	.917	.921	.924	.927	.930	.933	.936	.938	.941	.944
	3	.868	.872	.877	.882	.886	.891	.895	.899	.903	.907	.911
	4	.819	.825	.831	.837	.843	.849	.854	.860	.865	.870	.875
	5	.768	.775	.782	.789	.796	.803	.810	.816	.823	.829	.835
	6	.714	.722	.730	.738	.746	.755	.762	.769	.777	.784	.791
	7	.658	.666	.675	.684	.693	.702	.710	.718	.726	.735	.743
	8	.598	.607	.617	.626	.635	.645	.654	.663	.671	.681	.689
	9	.536	.545	.555	.564	.573	.584	.593	.602	.611	.621	.630
	10	.470	.479	.489	.498	.507	.518	.527	.536	.545	.555	.564
	11	.401	.409	.419	.427	.436	.447	.456	.464	.473	.483	.492
	12	.328	.336	.344	.352	.360	.370	.379	.386	.394	.404	.412
	13	.252	.258	.265	.272	.279	.288	.295	.301	.308	.317	.324
	14	.172	.176	.182	.186	.192	.199	.204	.208	.214	.221	.226
	15	.088	.089	.093	.094	.098	.103	.106	.108	.111	.116	.119
17	1	.962	.963	.965	.967	.968	.970	.971	.972	.974	.975	.976
	2	.921	.925	.928	.931	.934	.937	.940	.943	.945	.948	.950
	3	.879	.884	.888	.893	.898	.902	.906	.910	.914	.918	.921
	4	.834	.841	.846	.852	.858	.864	.869	.874	.880	.885	.889
	5	.788	.795	.802	.809	.816	.823	.829	.836	.842	.849	.854
	6	.738	.747	.755	.763	.771	.779	.786	.794	.801	.809	.815
	7	.687	.696	.704	.713	.723	.732	.740	.748	.757	.765	.772
	8	.632	.642	.651	.661	.671	.680	.689	.698	.708	.717	.724
	9	.575	.585	.595	.605	.615	.625	.634	.644	.654	.663	.672
	10	.515	.525	.535	.545	.556	.566	.575	.585	.596	.605	.614
	11	.452	.462	.471	.481	.492	.502	.511	.521	.531	.541	.549
	12	.385	.395	.403	.413	.423	.433	.441	.451	.461	.471	.479
	13	.316	.324	.331	.340	.350	.359	.366	.375	.385	.393	.400
	14	.242	.249	.255	.262	.271	.278	.284	.292	.301	.308	.314
	15	.165	.170	.174	.179	.186	.192	.196	.202	.209	.215	.218
	16	.084	.087	.088	.091	.096	.099	.100	.103	.109	.112	.113

APPENDIX A-4

Mortgage, Contract, or Loan Balance Table

ORIGINAL PERIOD (YEARS)	AGE (YEARS)	BALANCE OWED AS A RATIO OF ORIGINAL AMOUNT FOR VARIOUS INTEREST RATES										
		5%	5½%	6%	6½%	7%	7½%	8%	8½%	9%	9½%	10%
18	1	.965	.966	.968	.970	.971	.973	.974	.975	.977	.978	.979
	2	.928	.931	.934	.937	.940	.943	.946	.948	.951	.954	.956
	3	.889	.894	.898	.903	.907	.911	.916	.919	.923	.927	.930
	4	.848	.854	.860	.866	.872	.877	.883	.887	.892	.898	.902
	5	.805	.812	.819	.827	.833	.840	.847	.853	.859	.865	.871
	6	.759	.768	.776	.785	.793	.801	.808	.815	.822	.830	.837
	7	.712	.721	.730	.740	.749	.758	.766	.774	.782	.791	.798
	8	.662	.672	.682	.692	.702	.712	.721	.730	.738	.748	.756
	9	.609	.620	.630	.641	.651	.662	.672	.681	.690	.701	.710
	10	.554	.565	.576	.587	.597	.609	.619	.628	.638	.649	.659
	11	.496	.507	.517	.529	.539	.551	.561	.571	.581	.592	.602
	12	.435	.446	.456	.467	.477	.489	.499	.508	.518	.529	.539
	13	.370	.381	.390	.401	.411	.422	.431	.440	.449	.461	.470
	14	.303	.312	.321	.330	.339	.349	.358	.366	.374	.385	.394
	15	.232	.240	.247	.255	.262	.271	.279	.285	.292	.302	.309
	16	.157	.164	.168	.175	.180	.188	.193	.197	.203	.210	.216
	17	.079	.083	.085	.090	.092	.097	.101	.101	.104	.110	.113
19	1	.968	.969	.971	.972	.974	.975	.977	.978	.979	.980	.981
	2	.933	.937	.940	.943	.946	.948	.951	.954	.956	.959	.961
	3	.898	.903	.907	.912	.915	.920	.924	.927	.931	.935	.938
	4	.860	.866	.872	.878	.883	.888	.894	.899	.904	.909	.913
	5	.820	.828	.835	.842	.848	.855	.862	.868	.874	.880	.885
	6	.779	.788	.795	.804	.811	.819	.827	.834	.841	.848	.854
	7	.735	.745	.753	.763	.771	.780	.789	.797	.806	.813	.820
	8	.689	.700	.709	.720	.729	.738	.748	.757	.766	.775	.783
	9	.640	.652	.662	.673	.683	.693	.704	.713	.724	.733	.741
	10	.590	.602	.612	.624	.634	.644	.656	.666	.677	.687	.695
	11	.536	.549	.558	.571	.581	.592	.603	.614	.626	.636	.645
	12	.480	.492	.502	.515	.524	.535	.547	.558	.570	.580	.589
	13	.421	.433	.442	.455	.464	.474	.486	.497	.508	.519	.527
	14	.359	.370	.378	.391	.399	.409	.420	.430	.441	.451	.459
	15	.293	.304	.311	.322	.329	.338	.348	.357	.368	.377	.384
	16	.225	.234	.239	.249	.254	.262	.271	.278	.288	.295	.301
	17	.153	.160	.163	.171	.174	.179	.189	.192	.200	.206	.209
	18	.077	.082	.082	.088	.088	.091	.096	.099	.104	.107	.107

APPENDIX A-5

Mortgage, Contract, or Loan Balance Table

ORIGINAL PERIOD (YEARS)	AGE (YEARS)	BALANCE OWED AS A RATIO OF ORIGINAL AMOUNT FOR VARIOUS INTEREST RATES										
		5%	5½%	6%	6½%	7%	7½%	8%	8½%	9%	9½%	10%
20	1	.970	.972	.973	.975	.976	.976	.979	.980	.981	.982	.983
	2	.939	.942	.945	.948	.951	.953	.956	.958	.961	.963	.965
	3	.906	.910	.915	.919	.923	.927	.931	.935	.938	.941	.945
	4	.871	.877	.883	.888	.894	.899	.904	.909	.914	.918	.922
	5	.835	.842	.849	.856	.862	.869	.875	.881	.887	.892	.897
	6	.796	.805	.812	.821	.828	.836	.843	.851	.858	.864	.870
	7	.756	.765	.774	.783	.792	.801	.809	.818	.825	.832	.840
	8	.713	.724	.733	.744	.753	.763	.772	.782	.790	.798	.806
	9	.669	.680	.690	.701	.711	.722	.732	.742	.752	.760	.769
	10	.622	.634	.644	.656	.666	.678	.688	.700	.710	.719	.728
	11	.573	.585	.596	.608	.619	.631	.641	.653	.664	.673	.683
	12	.521	.533	.544	.556	.567	.579	.590	.603	.613	.622	.633
	13	.467	.478	.489	.501	.512	.524	.535	.547	.558	.568	.578
	14	.410	.421	.431	.442	.453	.465	.475	.488	.498	.507	.517
	15	.350	.360	.369	.380	.389	.401	.411	.422	.432	.440	.450
	16	.286	.295	.303	.313	.321	.332	.341	.351	.360	.367	.376
	17	.220	.227	.233	.242	.248	.257	.265	.274	.282	.287	.294
	18	.150	.155	.159	.166	.170	.177	.182	.190	.195	.198	.203
	19	.077	.080	.081	.085	.086	.091	.093	.099	.101	.101	.103
21	1	.972	.974	.975	.977	.978	.980	.981	.982	.983	.984	.985
	2	.943	.946	.949	.952	.955	.957	.960	.962	.965	.967	.969
	3	.913	.917	.922	.926	.930	.934	.937	.941	.944	.948	.951
	4	.881	.887	.892	.898	.903	.908	.913	.918	.922	.927	.931
	5	.847	.854	.861	.868	.874	.880	.887	.892	.898	.903	.909
	6	.811	.820	.828	.836	.843	.851	.858	.865	.872	.878	.885
	7	.774	.784	.793	.801	.810	.818	.827	.835	.843	.850	.858
	8	.735	.745	.756	.765	.775	.784	.793	.802	.811	.819	.828
	9	.693	.705	.716	.726	.737	.747	.757	.767	.777	.786	.795
	10	.650	.662	.674	.685	.696	.706	.718	.728	.739	.749	.759
	11	.605	.617	.629	.640	.652	.663	.675	.686	.697	.708	.719
	12	.557	.570	.582	.593	.605	.617	.629	.640	.652	.663	.675
	13	.506	.519	.531	.543	.555	.566	.579	.590	.603	.614	.626
	14	.453	.466	.478	.489	.501	.512	.525	.536	.548	.559	.572
	15	.398	.410	.421	.431	.443	.454	.466	.477	.489	.500	.512
	16	.339	.351	.361	.370	.381	.391	.403	.412	.424	.434	.446
	17	.278	.288	.297	.305	.315	.323	.334	.342	.353	.362	.374

APPENDICES

APPENDIX A–6

Mortgage, Contract, or Loan Balance Table

ORIGINAL PERIOD (YEARS)	AGE (YEARS)	BALANCE OWED AS A RATIO OF ORIGINAL AMOUNT FOR VARIOUS INTEREST RATES										
		5%	5½%	6%	6½%	7%	7½%	8%	8½%	9%	9½%	10%
21	18	.213	.222	.229	.235	.243	.250	.253	.266	.276	.283	.293
	19	.145	.152	.157	.161	.167	.171	.178	.183	.191	.196	.204
	20	.074	.078	.081	.081	.085	.086	.091	.093	.098	.101	.106
22	1	.974	.976	.977	.979	.980	.981	.983	.984	.985	.986	.987
	2	.947	.950	.953	.956	.959	.961	.964	.966	.968	.970	.972
	3	.919	.924	.928	.932	.936	.940	.943	.947	.950	.953	.956
	4	.889	.895	.901	.906	.911	.916	.921	.926	.930	.934	.938
	5	.858	.865	.872	.879	.885	.891	.897	.903	.908	.913	.918
	6	.825	.834	.841	.850	.857	.864	.872	.878	.884	.891	.896
	7	.790	.800	.809	.818	.827	.835	.844	.851	.858	.865	.872
	8	.754	.765	.774	.785	.794	.803	.813	.821	.829	.838	.845
	9	.715	.727	.737	.749	.759	.770	.780	.789	.798	.808	.816
	10	.675	.688	.699	.711	.722	.733	.745	.754	.764	.774	.783
	11	.633	.646	.657	.671	.682	.694	.706	.716	.726	.738	.748
	12	.588	.602	.613	.628	.639	.651	.664	.675	.686	.697	.708
	13	.541	.556	.567	.582	.593	.606	.619	.630	.641	.653	.664
	14	.492	.507	.517	.532	.544	.556	.570	.581	.592	.605	.616
	15	.441	.455	.465	.480	.491	.503	.517	.527	.538	.551	.562
	16	.386	.400	.409	.424	.434	.446	.460	.469	.480	.492	.505
	17	.329	.342	.350	.364	.373	.384	.398	.406	.417	.428	.437
	18	.269	.281	.287	.300	.308	.318	.330	.337	.346	.357	.365
	19	.206	.216	.221	.232	.238	.246	.257	.262	.269	.279	.286
	20	.140	.148	.150	.160	.163	.169	.178	.181	.185	.193	.197
	21	.070	.075	.075	.082	.083	.086	.093	.092	.093	.099	.100
23	1	.976	.978	.979	.980	.982	.983	.984	.985	.986	.987	.988
	2	.951	.954	.957	.960	.962	.965	.967	.969	.971	.973	.975
	3	.925	.929	.934	.937	.941	.945	.949	.951	.955	.958	.961
	4	.897	.903	.909	.914	.919	.924	.929	.932	.937	.941	.944
	5	.868	.875	.882	.888	.895	.901	.907	.912	.917	.923	.927
	6	.837	.845	.854	.861	.869	.876	.883	.889	.895	.902	.907
	7	.805	.814	.824	.832	.842	.849	.858	.864	.872	.880	.886
	8	.771	.782	.792	.801	.812	.821	.830	.838	.846	.855	.862
	9	.736	.747	.759	.769	.780	.790	.800	.808	.818	.828	.835
	10	.698	.710	.723	.733	.746	.756	.768	.777	.787	.798	.806
	11	.659	.672	.685	.696	.710	.720	.733	.742	.753	.766	.774

APPENDIX A-7

Mortgage, Contract, or Loan Balance Table

ORIGINAL PERIOD (YEARS)	AGE (YEARS)	BALANCE OWED AS A RATIO OF ORIGINAL AMOUNT FOR VARIOUS INTEREST RATES										
		5%	5½%	6%	6½%	7%	7½%	8%	8½%	9%	9½%	10%
23	12	.618	.631	.645	.656	.670	.682	.695	.704	.716	.730	.738
	13	.574	.588	.602	.613	.628	.640	.654	.664	.676	.690	.699
	14	.529	.542	.557	.568	.583	.595	.609	.619	.632	.647	.656
	15	.481	.494	.509	.519	.535	.546	.561	.571	.584	.599	.608
	16	.430	.443	.457	.468	.483	.494	.509	.518	.531	.546	.555
	17	.377	.389	.403	.412	.428	.438	.453	.460	.473	.489	.496
	18	.321	.332	.346	.354	.368	.377	.391	.398	.410	.425	.432
	19	.263	.272	.284	.291	.304	.312	.325	.329	.341	.355	.360
	20	.201	.209	.219	.224	.236	.241	.253	.256	.265	.279	.281
	21	.137	.142	.150	.152	.162	.166	.175	.175	.182	.194	.194
	22	.069	.071	.077	.076	.084	.084	.091	.087	.092	.102	.098
24	1	.978	.979	.981	.982	.983	.984	.986	.987	.988	.989	.989
	2	.955	.957	.960	.963	.965	.968	.970	.972	.974	.976	.978
	3	.930	.934	.939	.942	.946	.950	.953	.956	.959	.962	.965
	4	.904	.910	.916	.921	.926	.930	.934	.939	.943	.947	.950
	5	.877	.884	.891	.897	.904	.909	.915	.920	.925	.930	.934
	6	.849	.857	.865	.872	.880	.887	.893	.899	.906	.912	.917
	7	.819	.828	.838	.846	.855	.862	.870	.877	.885	.882	.898
	8	.788	.797	.808	.818	.827	.835	.844	.853	.861	.869	.876
	9	.755	.765	.777	.788	.798	.808	.817	.826	.836	.845	.853
	10	.720	.731	.744	.755	.767	.778	.787	.797	.808	.818	.827
	11	.684	.695	.709	.721	.733	.745	.755	.766	.778	.789	.798
	12	.645	.657	.672	.684	.697	.709	.720	.732	.745	.756	.766
	13	.605	.617	.633	.645	.659	.671	.682	.695	.708	.721	.731
	14	.563	.575	.591	.603	.617	.630	.642	.654	.669	.681	.692
	15	.518	.530	.546	.559	.573	.586	.597	.610	.625	.638	.649
	16	.471	.483	.499	.511	.526	.539	.550	.563	.578	.591	.602
	17	.422	.433	.449	.461	.475	.487	.498	.510	.526	.539	.549
	18	.370	.380	.396	.407	.420	.432	.442	.454	.469	.482	.492
	19	.316	.324	.339	.349	.361	.372	.381	.392	.406	.419	.428
	20	.259	.265	.279	.287	.298	.308	.315	.325	.338	.350	.357
	21	.199	.203	.216	.222	.231	.239	.243	.252	.264	.274	.279
	22	.136	.137	.148	.152	.159	.164	.166	.172	.183	.190	.193
	23	.069	.068	.076	.077	.081	.084	.082	.086	.094	.098	.098

APPENDIX A-8

Mortgage, Contract, or Loan Balance Table

ORIGINAL PERIOD (YEARS)	AGE (YEARS)	BALANCE OWED AS A RATIO OF ORIGINAL AMOUNT FOR VARIOUS INTEREST RATES										
		5%	5½%	6%	6½%	7%	7½%	8%	8½%	9%	9½%	10%
25	1	.979	.981	.982	.983	.985	.986	.987	.988	.989	.990	.990
	2	.958	.960	.963	.966	.968	.971	.973	.975	.976	.978	.980
	3	.935	.939	.943	.947	.951	.954	.957	.960	.963	.966	.968
	4	.911	.916	.922	.927	.932	.936	.941	.944	.948	.952	.956
	5	.886	.892	.899	.905	.911	.917	.923	.927	.932	.937	.941
	6	.859	.867	.875	.882	.890	.897	.903	.909	.914	.921	.926
	7	.831	.840	.849	.858	.866	.875	.882	.888	.895	.902	.908
	8	.802	.812	.822	.831	.841	.851	.859	.866	.874	.882	.889
	9	.771	.782	.793	.804	.815	.825	.834	.842	.851	.860	.868
	10	.739	.750	.762	.774	.786	.797	.807	.816	.826	.836	.845
	11	.705	.717	.730	.742	.755	.767	.778	.788	.798	.810	.819
	12	.669	.681	.695	.708	.722	.735	.747	.757	.768	.780	.791
	13	.631	.644	.659	.672	.687	.700	.713	.723	.735	.748	.759
	14	.592	.605	.620	.633	.649	.663	.676	.687	.699	.713	.725
	15	.550	.563	.578	.592	.608	.622	.635	.647	.659	.674	.686
	16	.506	.519	.534	.548	.564	.579	.592	.603	.616	.632	.644
	17	.460	.473	.488	.501	.518	.532	.545	.556	.569	.585	.597
	18	.412	.424	.438	.451	.467	.482	.494	.505	.517	.533	.546
	19	.361	.372	.386	.398	.414	.427	.439	.449	.461	.476	.488
	20	.308	.317	.330	.341	.356	.369	.380	.388	.399	.414	.425
	21	.252	.260	.271	.280	.294	.306	.315	.321	.331	.346	.356
	22	.193	.199	.208	.216	.228	.237	.245	.249	.257	.270	.279
	23	.131	.134	.141	.147	.157	.164	.169	.171	.176	.188	.194
	24	.066	.066	.070	.073	.080	.085	.087	.085	.088	.097	.100
30	2	.970	.972	.975	.977	.979	.981	.983	.984	.986	.987	.988
	4	.936	.941	.946	.950	.954	.958	.962	.965	.968	.971	.974
	6	.899	.907	.914	.920	.926	.932	.938	.943	.948	.952	.956
	8	.858	.868	.877	.885	.894	.902	.910	.917	.923	.929	.935
	10	.813	.825	.836	.846	.857	.867	.877	.886	.894	.902	.909
	12	.763	.777	.790	.802	.814	.826	.838	.849	.858	.868	.877
	14	.708	.723	.738	.751	.765	.778	.793	.805	.816	.828	.837
	16	.647	.664	.679	.693	.709	.723	.739	.753	.766	.779	.790
	18	.580	.597	.613	.627	.644	.659	.677	.692	.705	.720	.732
	20	.505	.522	.538	.552	.569	.585	.603	.620	.633	.649	.661
	25	.283	.296	.307	.316	.330	.342	.360	.374	.384	.398	.407
	29	.061	.064	.066	.064	.069	.071	.081	.087	.086	.093	.091

B. MORTGAGE, CONTRACT, OR LOAN PAYMENT TABLES

These tables are used to determine the periodic payment for loans, mortgages, or contracts based upon the period in years and interest rate applicable.

In order to determine the magnitude of the periodic payment, the appropriate table must first be selected, depending upon whether periodic payments are made on a monthly, semiannual, or annual schedule. The appropriate factor is then selected from the table based upon the interest rate and the length of time in years of the loan, mortgage, or contract. This factor is multiplied by the total amount owed in order to determine the periodic payment amount.

APPENDIX B–1

Mortgage, Contract, or Loan Payment Table

MONTHLY PAYMENT AS A RATIO OF ORIGINAL AMOUNT

PERIOD (YEARS)	INTEREST RATE										
	5%	5½%	6%	6½%	7%	7½%	8%	8½%	9%	9½%	10%
1	.0856	.0858	.0861	.0863	.0866	.0868	.0870	.0873	.0875	.0877	.0880
2	.0439	.0441	.0444	.0446	.0448	.0450	.0453	.0455	.0457	.0460	.0462
3	.0300	.0302	.0305	.0307	.0309	.0312	.0314	.0316	.0318	.0321	.0323
4	.0231	.0233	.0235	.0238	.0240	.0242	.0245	.0247	.0249	.0252	.0254
5	.0189	.0192	.0194	.0196	.0199	.0201	.0203	.0206	.0208	.0211	.0213
6	.0162	.0164	.0166	.0169	.0171	.0173	.0176	.0178	.0181	.0183	.0186
7	.0142	.0144	.0147	.0149	.0151	.0154	.0156	.0159	.0161	.0164	.0167
8	.0127	.0129	.0132	.0134	.0137	.0139	.0142	.0144	.0147	.0150	.0152
9	.0116	.0118	.0121	.0123	.0126	.0128	.0131	.0133	.0136	.0139	.0141
10	.0107	.0109	.0112	.0114	.0117	.0119	.0122	.0124	.0127	.0130	.0133
11	.0099	.0102	.0104	.0107	.0109	.0112	.0115	.0117	.0120	.0123	.0126
12	.0093	.0096	.0098	.0101	.0103	.0106	.0109	.0112	.0114	.0117	.0120
13	.0088	.0090	.0093	.0096	.0098	.0101	.0104	.0107	.0109	.0112	.0115
14	.0083	.0086	.0089	.0091	.0094	.0097	.0100	.0102	.0105	.0108	.0111
15	.0080	.0082	.0085	.0088	.0090	.0093	.0096	.0099	.0102	.0105	.0108
16	.0076	.0079	.0082	.0084	.0087	.0090	.0093	.0096	.0099	.0102	.0105
17	.0073	.0076	.0079	.0082	.0084	.0087	.0090	.0093	.0096	.0099	.0103
18	.0071	.0074	.0076	.0079	.0082	.0085	.0088	.0091	.0094	.0097	.0100
19	.0069	.0071	.0074	.0077	.0080	.0083	.0086	.0089	.0092	.0095	.0099
20	.0066	.0069	.0072	.0075	.0078	.0081	.0084	.0087	.0090	.0094	.0097
21	.0065	.0067	.0070	.0073	.0076	.0079	.0083	.0086	.0089	.0092	.0096
22	.0063	.0066	.0069	.0072	.0075	.0078	.0081	.0084	.0088	.0091	.0094
23	.0062	.0064	.0067	.0070	.0073	.0077	.0080	.0083	.0086	.0090	.0093
24	.0060	.0063	.0066	.0069	.0072	.0075	.0079	.0082	.0085	.0089	.0092
25	.0059	.0062	.0065	.0068	.0071	.0074	.0078	.0081	.0084	.0088	.0091

APPENDIX B-2

Mortgage, Contract, or Loan Payment Table

SEMIANNUAL PAYMENT AS A RATIO OF ORIGINAL AMOUNT

PERIOD (YEARS)	INTEREST RATE										
	5%	5½%	6%	6½%	7%	7½%	8%	8½%	9%	9½%	10%
1	.5188	.5207	.5226	.5245	.5264	.5283	.5302	.5321	.5340	.5359	.5378
2	.2658	.2674	.2690	.2706	.2723	.2739	.2755	.2771	.2788	.2804	.2820
3	.1816	.1831	.1846	.1861	.1877	.1892	.1908	.1923	.1939	.1955	.1970
4	.1395	.1410	.1425	.1440	.1455	.1470	.1485	.1501	.1516	.1532	.1547
5	.1143	.1157	.1172	.1187	.1203	.1218	.1233	.1248	.1264	.1279	.1295
6	.0975	.0990	.1005	.1020	.1035	.1050	.1066	.1081	.1097	.1113	.1128
7	.0855	.0870	.0885	.0901	.0916	.0931	.0947	.0962	.0978	.0994	.1010
8	.0766	.0781	.0796	.0812	.0827	.0843	.0858	.0874	.0890	.0906	.0923
9	.0697	.0712	.0727	.0743	.0758	.0774	.0790	.0806	.0822	.0839	.0856
10	.0642	.0657	.0672	.0688	.0704	.0720	.0736	.0752	.0769	.0786	.0803
11	.0597	.0612	.0628	.0643	.0659	.0676	.0692	.0709	.0726	.0743	.0760
12	.0559	.0575	.0591	.0607	.0623	.0639	.0656	.0673	.0690	.0707	.0725
13	.0528	.0544	.0559	.0576	.0592	.0609	.0626	.0643	.0660	.0678	.0696
14	.0501	.0517	.0533	.0549	.0566	.0583	.0600	.0618	.0635	.0653	.0671
15	.0478	.0494	.0510	.0527	.0544	.0561	.0578	.0596	.0614	.0632	.0651
16	.0458	.0474	.0491	.0507	.0525	.0542	.0560	.0578	.0596	.0614	.0633
17	.0440	.0467	.0473	.0490	.0508	.0525	.0543	.0561	.0580	.0599	.0618
18	.0425	.0441	.0458	.0475	.0493	.0511	.0529	.0547	.0566	.0585	.0604
19	.0411	.0428	.0445	.0462	.0480	.0498	.0516	.0535	.0554	.0573	.0593
20	.0398	.0415	.0433	.0450	.0468	.0487	.0505	.0524	.0544	.0563	.0583
21	.0387	.0405	.0422	.0440	.0458	.0477	.0496	.0515	.0534	.0554	.0574
22	.0377	.0395	.0412	.0430	.0449	.0468	.0487	.0506	.0526	.0546	.0566
23	.0368	.0386	.0404	.0422	.0441	.0460	.0479	.0499	.0519	.0539	.0559
24	.0360	.0378	.0396	.0414	.0433	.0452	.0472	.0492	.0512	.0532	.0553
25	.0353	.0371	.0389	.0407	.0426	.0446	.0466	.0486	.0506	.0527	.0548

APPENDIX B-3

Mortgage, Contract, or Loan Payment Table

ANNUAL PAYMENT AS A RATIO OF ORIGINAL AMOUNT

PERIOD (YEARS)	INTEREST RATE										
	5%	5½%	6%	6½%	7%	7½%	8%	8½%	9%	9½%	10%
2	.5378	.5416	.5454	.5493	.5531	.5569	.5608	.5646	.5685	.5723	.5762
3	.3670	.3707	.3741	.3776	.3811	.3845	.3880	.3915	.3951	.3986	.4021
4	.2820	.2853	.2886	.2919	.2952	.2986	.3019	.3053	.3087	.3121	.3155
5	.2310	.2342	.2374	.2406	.2439	.2472	.2505	.2538	.2571	.2604	.2638
6	.1970	.2002	.2034	.2066	.2098	.2131	.2163	.2196	.2229	.2263	.2296
7	.1728	.1760	.1791	.1823	.1856	.1888	.1921	.1954	.1987	.2020	.2054
8	.1547	.1579	.1610	.1642	.1675	.1707	.1740	.1773	.1807	.1841	.1875
9	.1407	.1438	.1470	.1502	.1535	.1568	.1601	.1634	.1668	.1702	.1737
10	.1295	.1327	.1359	.1391	.1424	.1457	.1490	.1524	.1558	.1593	.1628
11	.1204	.1236	.1268	.1301	.1334	.1367	.1401	.1435	.1470	.1504	.1540
12	.1128	.1160	.1193	.1226	.1259	.1293	.1327	.1362	.1397	.1482	.1468
13	.1065	.1097	.1130	.1163	.1197	.1231	.1265	.1300	.1336	.1372	.1408
14	.1010	.1043	.1076	.1110	.1144	.1178	.1213	.1249	.1284	.1321	.1358
15	.0964	.0996	.1030	.1064	.1098	.1133	.1168	.1204	.1241	.1278	.1315
16	.0923	.0956	.0990	.1024	.1059	.1094	.1130	.1166	.1203	.1240	.1278
17	.0887	.0921	.0955	.0989	.1024	.1060	.1096	.1133	.1171	.1208	.1247
18	.0855	.0889	.0924	.0959	.0994	.1030	.1067	.1104	.1142	.1181	.1219
19	.0828	.0862	.0896	.0932	.0968	.1004	.1041	.1079	.1117	.1156	.1196
20	.0803	.0837	.0872	.0908	.0944	.0981	.1019	.1057	.1096	.1135	.1175
21	.0780	.0815	.0850	.0886	.0923	.0960	.0998	.1037	.1076	.1116	.1156
22	.0760	.0795	.0831	.0867	.0904	.0942	.0980	.1019	.1059	.1099	.1140
23	.0741	.0777	.0813	.0850	.0887	.0925	.0964	.1004	.1044	.1085	.1126
24	.0725	.0760	.0797	.0834	.0872	.0911	.0950	.0990	.1030	.1071	.1113
25	.0710	.0746	.0782	.0820	.0858	.0897	.0937	.0977	.1018	.1060	.1102
26	.0696	.0732	.0769	.0807	.0846	.0885	.0925	.0966	.1007	.1049	.1092

C. THE EFFECT OF DIFFERENT CAPITAL GAINS TAX RATE ASSUMPTIONS ON PROFITABILITY ANALYSIS CHARTS DATA OF CHAPTERS 5 AND 7

The profitability analysis charts for rental houses and apartment houses (Chapters 5 and 7, respectively) assume a capital gains tax rate of 20 percent, the rate in effect at the time of this writing. Recognizing the susceptibility to change of this rate under changing political and economic conditions, the tables in this appendix are provided. The tables indicate the *changes* or *deltas* in internal rate of return (IRR) from that indicated in the profitability analysis charts of Chapters 5 and 7, under the alternative assumptions of 10 percent and 0 percent capital gains tax rates. To use the tables, locate the worksheet number in the tables that corresponds to that of the applicable chart of Chapter 5 or 7, and which reflects the desired alternative capital gains tax rate, and add the incremental IRR percentage shown in the table to that indicated by the profitability chart of Chapter 5 or 7.

For example, referring to the chart identified as Worksheet 5-1 in the chart section at the end of Chapter 5, the IRR is about 21 percent for a rental house for which the monthly rent as a percent of price is 0.8 and the annual appreciation rate is 10 percent. If the capital gains tax is 10 percent, rather than the 20 percent reflected in the Chapter 5 charts, Worksheet 5-1 table in this appendix indicates that the IRR would increase by 2.6 percentage points, resulting in an IRR of 23.6 percent (21 percent plus 2.6 percent).

APPENDIX C–1

Rental Houses: Capital Gains Tax Variations

Base IRR's are at a 20% Capital Gains Tax

| | Changes from Base IRR's (%) for Capital Gains Tax of 10% | | | | | Changes from Base IRR's (%) for Capital Gains Tax of 0% | | | | |

Worksheet 5-1 Delta IRR's for: 3 Yr Hold, 28% Tax Bracket, 6% Interest Rate

Rent / Price, %	0.4	0.6	0.8	1.0	1.2	0.4	0.6	0.8	1.0	1.2
0	-0.8	-0.7	-0.7	-0.6	-0.5	-1.6	-1.5	-1.3	-1.2	-1.0
Appreciation 5	1.6	1.5	1.4	1.3	1.2	3.2	3.0	2.8	2.6	2.5
Rates, % 10	2.9	2.8	2.6	2.5	2.4	5.7	5.5	5.2	4.9	4.7
15	3.8	3.7	3.5	3.4	3.2	7.5	7.2	6.9	6.6	6.3
20	4.6	4.4	4.2	4.1	3.9	8.9	8.6	8.3	8.0	7.7

Worksheet 5-2 Delta IRR's for: 5 Yr Hold, 28% Tax Bracket, 6% Interest Rate

Rent / Price, %	0.4	0.6	0.8	1.0	1.2	0.4	0.6	0.8	1.0	1.2
0	0.4	0.3	0.3	0.2	0.2	0.8	0.7	0.6	0.5	0.4
Appreciation 5	1.9	1.7	1.5	1.4	1.2	3.7	3.3	3.0	2.7	2.4
Rates, % 10	2.5	2.3	2.1	1.9	1.8	4.8	4.5	4.1	3.8	3.4
15	2.9	2.7	2.5	2.3	2.1	5.6	5.2	4.8	4.5	4.2
20	3.2	3.0	2.8	2.6	2.5	6.1	5.8	5.4	5.1	4.7

Worksheet 5-3 Delta IRR's for: 10 Yr Hold, 28% Tax Bracket, 6% Interest Rate

Rent / Price, %	0.4	0.6	0.8	1.0	1.2	0.4	0.6	0.8	1.0	1.2
0	1.2	0.9	0.7	0.5	0.4	2.3	1.8	1.3	1.0	0.7
Appreciation 5	1.5	1.8	1.0	0.8	0.7	2.8	2.9	2.0	1.6	1.3
Rates, % 10	1.5	1.3	1.1	1.0	0.8	2.9	2.5	2.2	1.8	1.5
15	1.6	1.4	1.2	1.0	0.9	3.0	2.7	2.3	2.0	1.7
20	1.7	1.5	1.3	1.1	0.9	3.1	2.8	2.5	2.1	1.8

Worksheet 5-4 Delta IRR's for: 3 Yr Hold, 28% Tax Bracket, 9% Interest Rate

Rent / Price, %	0.4	0.6	0.8	1.0	1.2	0.4	0.6	0.8	1.0	1.2
0	-1.0	-0.9	-0.8	-0.7	-0.6	-2.0	-1.7	-1.5	-1.3	-1.2
Appreciation 5	1.8	1.7	1.6	1.5	1.3	3.6	3.3	3.1	2.9	2.7
Rates, % 10	3.1	3.0	2.8	2.7	2.5	6.1	5.8	5.5	5.2	4.9
15	4.0	3.8	3.7	3.5	3.4	7.8	7.5	7.2	6.9	6.6
20	4.7	4.6	4.4	4.2	4.1	9.2	8.9	8.5	8.2	7.9

Worksheet 5-5 Delta IRR's for: 5 Yr Hold, 28% Tax Bracket, 9% Interest Rate

Rent / Price, %	0.4	0.6	0.8	1.0	1.2	0.4	0.6	0.8	1.0	1.2
0	0.6	0.5	0.4	0.3	0.2	1.2	0.9	0.7	0.6	0.5
Appreciation 5	2.2	2.0	1.7	1.6	1.4	4.2	3.8	3.4	3.0	2.7
Rates, % 10	2.7	2.5	2.3	2.1	1.9	5.2	4.8	4.4	4.1	3.7
15	3.1	2.9	2.7	2.5	2.3	5.9	5.5	5.1	4.8	4.4
20	3.3	2.9	2.7	2.5	2.3	6.3	6.0	5.6	5.3	5.0

Worksheet 5-6 Delta IRR's for: 10 Yr Hold, 28% Tax Bracket, 9% Interest Rate

Rent / Price, %	0.4	0.6	0.8	1.0	1.2	0.4	0.6	0.8	1.0	1.2
0	2.0	1.5	1.1	0.8	0.5	3.8	2.9	2.1	1.5	1.0
Appreciation 5	1.7	1.4	1.2	1.0	0.8	3.2	2.7	2.3	1.9	1.5
Rates, % 10	1.7	1.5	1.3	1.1	0.9	3.2	2.8	2.4	2.0	1.7
15	1.7	1.5	1.3	1.1	0.9	3.2	2.8	2.5	2.2	1.8
20	1.7	1.5	1.4	1.2	1.0	3.2	2.9	2.6	2.3	1.9

APPENDIX C–2

Rental Houses: Capital Gains Tax Variations

Base IRR's are at a 20% Capital Gains Tax

| | Changes from Base IRR's (%) for Capital Gains Tax of 10% | | | | | Changes from Base IRR's (%) for Capital Gains Tax of 0% | | | | |

Worksheet 5-7   Delta IRR's for: 3 Yr Hold, 36% Tax Bracket, 6% Interest Rate

Rent / Price, %	0.4	0.6	0.8	1.0	1.2	0.4	0.6	0.8	1.0	1.2
0	-0.8	-0.7	-0.6	-0.6	-0.5	-1.6	-1.4	-1.3	-1.2	-1.1
Appreciation 5	1.6	1.5	1.4	1.3	1.3	3.2	3.0	2.8	2.6	2.5
Rates, % 10	2.9	2.8	2.6	2.5	2.4	5.7	5.4	5.2	4.9	4.7
15	3.8	3.7	3.5	3.4	3.8	7.4	7.1	6.9	6.6	6.9
20	4.5	4.4	4.2	4.1	4.0	8.8	8.5	8.3	8.0	7.7

Worksheet 5-8   Delta IRR's for: 5 Yr Hold, 36% Tax Bracket, 6% Interest Rate

Rent / Price, %	0.4	0.6	0.8	1.0	1.2	0.4	0.6	0.8	1.0	1.2
0	0.4	0.3	0.3	0.2	0.2	0.8	0.7	0.6	14.3	0.4
Appreciation 5	1.9	1.7	1.5	1.4	1.2	3.6	3.3	3.0	2.7	2.4
Rates, % 10	2.5	2.3	2.1	2.0	1.8	4.8	4.4	4.1	3.8	3.5
15	2.9	2.7	2.5	2.4	2.2	5.5	5.2	4.8	4.5	4.2
20	3.1	3.0	2.8	2.7	2.5	6.0	5.7	5.4	5.1	4.8

Worksheet 5-9   Delta IRR's for: 10 Yr Hold, 36% Tax Bracket, 6% Interest Rate

Rent / Price, %	0.4	0.6	0.8	1.0	1.2	0.4	0.6	0.8	1.0	1.2
0	1.1	0.9	0.7	0.5	0.4	2.2	1.7	1.3	1.0	0.7
Appreciation 5	1.4	1.2	1.0	0.8	0.7	2.7	2.3	2.0	1.6	1.3
Rates, % 10	1.5	1.3	1.2	1.0	0.8	2.9	2.5	2.2	1.9	1.6
15	1.6	1.4	1.2	1.1	0.9	3.0	2.7	2.4	2.1	1.8
20	1.6	1.5	1.3	1.1	1.0	3.1	2.8	2.5	2.2	1.9

Worksheet 5-10   Delta IRR's for: 3 Yr Hold, 36% Tax Bracket, 9% Interest Rate

Rent / Price, %	0.4	0.6	0.8	1.0	1.2	0.4	0.6	0.8	1.0	1.2
0	-0.9	-0.8	-0.7	-0.7	-0.6	-1.9	-1.7	-1.5	-1.3	-1.2
Appreciation 5	1.8	1.6	1.5	1.4	1.4	3.5	3.2	3.0	2.8	2.7
Rates, % 10	3.1	2.9	2.8	2.6	2.5	6.0	5.7	5.4	5.2	4.9
15	4.0	3.8	3.7	3.5	3.4	7.7	7.4	7.1	6.9	6.6
20	4.7	4.5	4.4	4.2	4.1	9.1	8.8	8.5	8.2	8.0

Worksheet 5-11   Delta IRR's for: 5 Yr Hold, 36% Tax Bracket, 9% Interest Rate

Rent / Price, %	0.4	0.6	0.8	1.0	1.2	0.4	0.6	0.8	1.0	1.2
0	0.5	0.4	0.4	0.3	0.2	1.1	0.9	0.7	0.6	0.5
Appreciation 5	2.1	1.9	1.7	1.5	1.4	4.1	3.7	3.3	3.0	2.7
Rates, % 10	2.7	2.5	2.3	2.1	1.9	5.1	4.7	4.4	4.1	3.8
15	3.0	2.8	2.6	2.5	2.3	5.8	5.4	5.1	4.8	4.5
20	3.3	3.1	2.9	2.8	2.6	6.3	5.9	5.6	5.3	5.0

Worksheet 5-12   Delta IRR's for: 10 Yr Hold, 36% Tax Bracket, 9% Interest Rate

Rent / Price, %	0.4	0.6	0.8	1.0	1.2	0.4	0.6	0.8	1.0	1.2
0	1.8	1.4	1.0	0.7	0.5	3.4	2.6	1.9	1.4	1.0
Appreciation 5	1.6	1.4	1.2	1.0	0.8	3.1	2.7	2.3	1.9	1.5
Rates, % 10	1.6	1.4	1.3	1.1	0.9	3.1	2.7	2.4	2.1	1.8
15	1.7	1.5	1.3	1.1	1.0	3.1	2.8	2.5	2.2	1.9
20	1.7	1.5	1.4	1.2	1.0	3.2	2.9	2.6	2.3	2.0

APPENDIX C-3

Apartment Houses: Capital Gains Tax Variations

Base IRR's at 20% Capital Gains Tax

Changes from Base IRR's (%) for Capital Gains Tax of 10%	Changes from Base IRR's (%) for Capital Gains Tax of 0%

Worksheet 7-1   Delta IRR's for: 10 Yr Hold, 28% Tax Bracket, 6% Interest Rate, Appreciation Rate = 0%

Price / Gross Income:		4	6	8	10	12		4	6	8	10	12
	0.2	0.10	0.28	0.46	0.62	0.74		0.19	0.54	0.89	1.20	1.44
Expense to	0.3	0.14	0.36	0.55	0.71	0.84		0.27	0.70	1.08	1.38	1.62
Income Ratio:	0.4	0.21	0.46	0.66	0.82	0.93		0.42	0.89	1.28	1.58	1.80
	0.5	0.31	0.59	0.79	0.93	1.04		0.61	1.14	1.52	1.80	2.00

Worksheet 7-2   Delta IRR's for: 10 Yr Hold, 28% Tax Bracket, 6% Interest Rate, Appreciation Rate = 5%

Price / Gross Income:		4	6	8	10	12		4	6	8	10	12
	0.2	0.21	0.49	0.71	0.86	0.97		0.42	0.95	1.37	1.67	1.88
Expense to	0.3	0.29	0.59	0.80	0.95	1.05		0.57	1.15	1.55	1.82	2.02
Income Ratio:	0.4	0.40	0.71	0.90	1.03	1.12		0.78	1.37	1.74	1.98	2.16
	0.5	0.54	0.83	1.01	1.12	1.21		1.05	1.61	1.94	2.16	2.31

Worksheet 7-3   Delta IRR's for: 10 Yr Hold, 28% Tax Bracket, 6% Interest Rate, Appreciation Rate = 10%

Price / Gross Income:		4	6	8	10	12		4	6	8	10	12
	0.2	0.29	0.60	0.82	0.96	1.08		0.57	1.17	1.59	1.86	2.07
Expense to	0.3	0.37	0.71	0.91	1.05	1.14		0.75	1.38	1.76	2.01	2.19
Income Ratio:	0.4	0.50	0.82	1.01	1.13	1.20		0.99	1.59	1.95	2.17	2.31
	0.5	0.65	0.94	1.11	1.20	1.28		1.27	1.82	2.13	2.31	2.44

Worksheet 7-4   Delta IRR's for: 10 Yr Hold, 28% Tax Bracket, 6% Interest Rate, Appreciation Rate = 15%

Price / Gross Income:		4	6	8	10	12		4	6	8	10	12
	0.2	-0.05	0.68	0.90	1.04	1.14		0.29	1.32	1.74	2.01	2.20
Expense to	0.3	0.45	0.79	0.98	1.12	1.21		0.89	1.53	1.90	2.16	2.32
Income Ratio:	0.4	0.58	0.90	1.09	1.18	1.27		1.13	1.74	2.09	2.28	2.44
	0.5	0.73	1.02	1.18	1.27	1.34		1.42	1.97	2.26	2.44	2.56

Worksheet 7-5   Delta IRR's for: 10 Yr Hold, 28% Tax Bracket, 6% Interest Rate, Appreciation Rate = 20%

Price / Gross Income:		4	6	8	10	12		4	6	8	10	12
	0.2	0.40	0.74	0.96	1.11	1.20		0.79	1.45	1.87	2.13	2.32
Expense to	0.3	0.52	0.85	1.05	1.18	1.27		1.01	1.65	2.03	2.27	2.44
Income Ratio:	0.4	0.64	0.96	1.14	1.26	1.33		1.26	1.88	2.20	2.41	2.55
	0.5	0.80	1.08	1.24	1.33	1.40		1.55	2.08	2.38	2.55	2.68

APPENDIX C–4

Apartment Houses: Capital Gains Tax Variations

Base IRR's at 20% Capital Gains Tax

Changes from Base IRR's (%) for Capital Gains Tax of 10%	Changes from Base IRR's (%) for Capital Gains Tax of 0%

Worksheet 7-6 Delta IRR's for: 10 Yr Hold, 28% Tax Bracket, 9% Interest Rate, Appreciation Rate = 0%

Price / Gross Income:		4	6	8	10	12	4	6	8	10	12
	0.2	0.13	0.38	0.67	0.94	1.16	0.26	0.76	1.31	1.81	2.22
Expense to	0.3	0.19	0.51	0.83	1.10	1.33	0.38	1.00	1.60	2.12	2.52
Income Ratio:	0.4	0.29	0.67	1.02	1.29	1.51	0.58	1.31	1.96	2.46	2.85
	0.5	0.45	0.89	1.35	1.51	1.70	0.88	1.71	2.37	2.85	3.20

Worksheet 7-7 Delta IRR's for: 10 Yr Hold, 28% Tax Bracket, 9% Interest Rate, Appreciation Rate = 5%

Price / Gross Income:		4	6	8	10	12	4	6	8	10	12
	0.2	0.26	0.59	0.85	1.03	1.16	0.51	1.15	1.64	1.97	2.22
Expense to	0.3	0.36	0.71	0.95	1.13	1.24	0.70	1.38	1.84	2.15	2.37
Income Ratio:	0.4	0.49	0.85	1.07	1.22	1.33	0.95	1.64	2.06	2.33	2.53
	0.5	0.65	0.99	1.20	1.33	1.42	1.26	1.91	2.29	2.53	2.70

Worksheet 7-8 Delta IRR's for: 10 Yr Hold, 28% Tax Bracket, 9% Interest Rate, Appreciation Rate = 10%

Price / Gross Income:		4	6	8	10	12	4	6	8	10	12
	0.2	0.34	0.68	0.92	1.08	1.18	0.67	1.33	1.78	2.07	2.27
Expense to	0.3	0.44	0.79	1.02	1.16	1.26	0.88	1.54	1.96	2.22	2.41
Income Ratio:	0.4	0.58	0.91	1.12	1.24	1.33	1.14	1.78	2.15	2.38	2.54
	0.5	0.74	1.06	1.22	1.33	1.41	1.43	2.03	2.34	2.54	2.68

Worksheet 7-9 Delta IRR's for: 10 Yr Hold, 28% Tax Bracket, 9% Interest Rate, Appreciation Rate = 15%

Price / Gross Income:		4	6	8	10	12	4	6	8	10	12
	0.2	0.40	0.76	0.98	1.12	1.23	0.79	1.46	1.89	2.16	2.35
Expense to	0.3	0.51	0.86	1.07	1.21	1.29	1.01	1.67	2.07	2.31	2.48
Income Ratio:	0.4	0.65	0.98	1.17	1.28	1.36	1.27	1.89	2.24	2.45	2.60
	0.5	0.81	1.10	1.26	1.36	1.43	1.56	2.12	2.41	2.60	2.72

Worksheet 7-10 Delta IRR's for: 10 Yr Hold, 28% Tax Bracket, 9% Interest Rate, Appreciation Rate = 20%

Price / Gross Income:		4	6	8	10	12	4	6	8	10	12
	0.2	0.45	0.81	1.03	1.18	1.28	0.88	1.57	1.99	2.26	2.45
Expense to	0.3	0.57	0.91	1.12	1.25	1.34	1.11	1.77	2.15	2.39	2.56
Income Ratio:	0.4	0.70	1.03	1.21	1.32	1.39	1.38	1.99	2.33	2.53	2.67
	0.5	0.86	1.15	1.31	1.39	1.47	1.67	2.21	2.50	2.67	2.80

APPENDIX C–5

Apartment Houses: Capital Gains Tax Variations

Base IRR's at 20% Capital Gains Tax

Changes from Base IRR's (%) for Capital Gains Tax of 10%	Changes from Base IRR's (%) for Capital Gains Tax of 0%

Worksheet 7-11   Delta IRR's for: 10 Yr Hold, 36% Tax Bracket, 6% Interest Rate, Appreciation Rate = 0%

Price / Gross Income:		4	6	8	10	12		4	6	8	10	12
	0.2	0.11	0.29	0.48	0.62	0.74		0.23	0.58	0.93	1.20	1.43
Expense to	0.3	0.17	0.38	0.56	0.70	0.82		0.33	0.75	1.09	1.37	1.58
Income Ratio:	0.4	0.24	0.48	0.67	0.81	0.90		0.47	0.93	1.29	1.55	1.74
	0.5	0.34	0.60	0.77	0.90	1.00		0.67	1.16	1.50	1.74	1.91

Worksheet 7-12   Delta IRR's for: 10 Yr Hold, 36% Tax Bracket, 6% Interest Rate, Appreciation Rate = 5%

Price / Gross Income:		4	6	8	10	12		4	6	8	10	12
	0.2	0.25	0.53	0.74	0.88	0.98		0.50	1.04	1.43	1.70	1.89
Expense to	0.3	0.33	0.63	0.83	0.96	1.05		0.66	1.23	1.60	1.85	2.01
Income Ratio:	0.4	0.45	0.74	0.92	1.03	1.11		0.88	1.43	1.77	1.99	2.14
	0.5	0.58	0.85	1.02	1.11	1.19		1.13	1.65	1.96	2.14	2.27

Worksheet 7-13   Delta IRR's for: 10 Yr Hold, 36% Tax Bracket, 6% Interest Rate, Appreciation Rate = 10%

Price / Gross Income:		4	6	8	10	12		4	6	8	10	12
	0.2	0.35	0.65	0.85	0.99	1.09		0.68	1.27	1.66	1.91	2.09
Expense to	0.3	0.44	0.75	0.95	1.07	1.15		0.87	1.46	1.82	2.05	2.20
Income Ratio:	0.4	0.56	0.85	1.03	1.13	1.21		1.10	1.66	1.99	2.18	2.32
	0.5	0.70	0.97	0.52	1.21	1.26		1.36	1.87	1.55	2.32	2.43

Worksheet 7-14   Delta IRR's for: 10 Yr Hold, 36% Tax Bracket, 6% Interest Rate, Appreciation Rate = 15%

Price / Gross Income:		4	6	8	10	12		4	6	8	10	12
	0.2	0.42	0.73	0.94	1.08	1.17		0.82	1.43	1.82	2.07	2.24
Expense to	0.3	0.52	0.83	1.02	1.14	1.22		1.02	1.62	1.97	2.20	2.35
Income Ratio:	0.4	0.64	0.94	1.11	1.22	1.29		1.25	1.82	2.14	2.33	2.46
	0.5	0.78	1.05	1.19	1.29	1.34		1.52	2.03	2.29	2.46	2.57

Worksheet 7-15   Delta IRR's for: 10 Yr Hold, 36% Tax Bracket, 6% Interest Rate, Appreciation Rate = 20%

Price / Gross Income:		4	6	8	10	12		4	6	8	10	12
	0.2	0.47	0.81	1.01	1.14	1.23		0.93	1.57	1.95	2.20	2.36
Expense to	0.3	0.59	0.91	1.09	1.21	1.29		1.15	1.76	2.11	2.32	2.48
Income Ratio:	0.4	0.71	1.01	1.17	1.28	1.35		1.39	1.95	2.26	2.46	2.58
	0.5	0.86	1.12	1.26	1.35	1.40		1.66	2.17	2.42	2.58	2.69

APPENDIX C–6

Apartment Houses: Capital Gains Tax Variations

	Base IRR's at 20% Capital Gains Tax
Changes from Base IRR's (%) for Capital Gains Tax of 10%	Changes from Base IRR's (%) for Capital Gains Tax of 0%

Worksheet 7-16   Delta IRR's for: 10 Yr Hold, 36% Tax Bracket, 9% Interest Rate, Appreciation Rate = 0%

Price / Gross Income:		4	6	8	10	12		4	6	8	10	12
	0.2	0.15	0.41	0.68	0.91	1.11		0.30	0.80	1.32	1.75	2.12
Expense to	0.3	0.22	0.52	0.81	1.06	1.24		0.44	1.03	1.57	2.02	2.37
Income Ratio:	0.4	0.32	0.68	0.98	1.22	1.40		0.63	1.32	1.88	2.32	2.65
	0.5	0.47	0.87	1.17	1.40	1.57		0.91	1.68	2.24	2.65	2.95

Worksheet 7-17   Delta IRR's for: 10 Yr Hold, 36% Tax Bracket, 9% Interest Rate, Appreciation Rate = 5%

Price / Gross Income:		4	6	8	10	12		4	6	8	10	12
	0.2	0.31	0.63	0.86	1.03	1.15		0.60	1.22	1.67	1.98	2.20
Expense to	0.3	0.40	0.74	0.97	1.12	1.23		0.79	1.44	1.86	2.14	2.34
Income Ratio:	0.4	0.53	0.86	1.07	1.21	1.30		1.03	1.67	2.06	2.31	2.48
	0.5	0.69	1.00	1.18	1.30	1.38		1.33	1.92	2.26	2.48	2.63

Worksheet 7-18   Delta IRR's for: 10 Yr Hold, 36% Tax Bracket, 9% Interest Rate, Appreciation Rate = 10%

Price / Gross Income:		4	6	8	10	12		4	6	8	10	12
	0.2	0.39	0.73	0.95	1.09	1.19		0.77	1.42	1.84	2.10	2.29
Expense to	0.3	0.51	0.83	1.04	1.17	1.26		0.99	1.62	2.00	2.24	2.41
Income Ratio:	0.4	0.63	0.95	1.13	1.25	1.33		1.22	1.84	2.17	2.38	2.53
	0.5	0.78	1.07	1.23	1.33	1.39		1.51	2.05	2.35	2.53	2.65

Worksheet 7-19   Delta IRR's for: 10 Yr Hold, 36% Tax Bracket, 9% Interest Rate, Appreciation Rate = 15%

Price / Gross Income:		4	6	8	10	12		4	6	8	10	12
	0.2	0.46	0.80	1.01	1.15	1.24		0.90	1.56	1.95	2.20	2.38
Expense to	0.3	0.58	0.91	1.10	1.22	1.30		1.13	1.75	2.11	2.33	2.49
Income Ratio:	0.4	0.70	1.01	1.18	1.29	1.36		1.37	1.95	2.27	2.47	2.60
	0.5	0.85	1.13	1.27	1.36	1.42		1.65	2.17	2.44	2.60	2.71

Worksheet 7-20   Delta IRR's for: 10 Yr Hold, 36% Tax Bracket, 9% Interest Rate, Appreciation Rate = 20%

Price / Gross Income:		4	6	8	10	12		4	6	8	10	12
	0.2	0.52	0.87	1.07	1.20	1.30		1.01	1.68	2.06	2.31	2.49
Expense to	0.3	0.63	0.97	1.15	1.27	1.35		1.24	1.87	2.22	2.44	2.58
Income Ratio:	0.4	0.77	1.07	1.23	1.33	1.40		1.50	2.06	2.37	2.56	2.68
	0.5	0.92	1.18	1.32	1.40	1.47		1.77	2.27	2.53	2.68	2.80

INDEX

ABOUT THE AUTHORS

William Benke retired following 40 years of management experience in strategic business planning, business analysis, and industrial engineering with the Boeing, Coca-Cola, Montgomery Ward, and Welch Grape Juice companies. His responsibilities included the financial analysis of new business opportunities and the direction of task force teams to develop business strategy and solutions to complex operating problems. He is a graduate of New York University with a degree in Administrative Engineering. His broad analytical skills extend to real estate investment analysis, the subject of this and two earlier books: *Land Investor's Profit Guide and Negotiating Manual* (Prentice Hall, 1973) and *All About Land Investment* (McGraw-Hill, 1976). He is also the author of *Church Wake-up Call* (Haworth Press, 2000). In addition to applying the analytical business techniques of the industrial world to real estate and other fields where it is often a missing discipline, he is active in civic/community volunteerism and has rendered organizational, analytical, and strategic planning assistance to such civic programs as the Seattle Opera, the Seattle Art Museum, the King Tutankhamun ("Tut") exhibit when it appeared in Seattle, Childhaven (rehabilitates abused and neglected children), and the Salvation Army.

Joseph M. Fowler passed away on May 24, 2001. He was an accomplished financial analysis professional. He retired from Boeing as Director of Financial Analysis, Asia Pacific area. After retirement, he provided management consulting services to international airlines in financial planning and equipment forecasting. He held both B.S. and M.S. degrees in Mechanical Engineering from Perdue University and an MBA from Seattle University. His financial analysis expertise has been applied in the development of the unique profitability analysis charts and tables included in this book. His other accomplishments in the business and technical fields include several engineering papers and special proprietary documents prepared for airlines, which provided extensive economic analyses and forecasts regarding equipment options and were important in multimillion-dollar aircraft purchase decisions. Mr. Fowler maintained an active interest in real estate investment and applied his extensive financial analysis skills to this area of investment, as well.